JESSICA SWALE

Jessica Swale is an award-winning writer and director. She trained at Central School of Speech and Drama and the University of Exeter.

Her plays include *Nell Gwynn*, which premiered at Shakespeare's Globe before transferring to the West End, and won the 2016 Oliver Award for Best New Comedy, and *Blue Stockings*, which won her a nomination for Most Promising Playwright in the Evening Standard Awards 2013. She is now writing the screenplay, and an original film, *Summerland*, after winning a JJ Screenwriting Bursary from BAFTA.

Jessica is Artistic Director of Red Handed Theatre Company, which is dedicated to creating new work and rediscovering forgotten plays. Recent productions include *The Rivals* starring Celia Imrie, the London premiere of *Palace of the End* by Judith Thompson, and the first major revival of Hannah Cowley's *The Belle's Stratagem*, which won her a nomination for Best Director at the Evening Standard Awards.

Other direction includes *Bedlam* (Shakespeare's Globe); *Sleuth* (Watermill); *Fallen Angels* (Salisbury Playhouse); *Winter* (TNL, Canada); *The Busy Body*, *Someone to Watch Over Me* (Southwark), *The School for Scandal* (Park Theatre); and productions at RADA and LAMDA. Jessica was Max Stafford-Clark's Associate Director at Out of Joint from 2007–2010.

Jessica is an associate artist with Youth Bridge Global, an international NGO which uses theatre as a tool for promoting social change in war-torn and developing nations. As such, she has lived in the Marshall Islands and in Bosnia and Herzegovina, directing Shakespeare productions including *The Comedy of Errors*, *Much Ado About Nothing*, *Twelfth Night* and *The Tempest*.

She has written two other titles in the *Drama Games* series: *for Devising*, and *for Rehearsals*.

drama games

A series of books for teachers, workshop leaders, directors and actors in need of new and dynamic activities when working in education, workshop or rehearsal.

Also available in this series
DRAMA GAMES FOR...

Chris Johnston
THOSE WHO LIKE TO SAY NO

Jessica Swale
DEVISING
REHEARSALS

Thomasina Unsworth
ACTORS

Katherine Zachest
YOUNG CHILDREN

*The publisher welcomes suggestions
for further titles in the series.*

Jessica Swale

drama games
FOR CLASSROOMS
AND WORKSHOPS

Foreword by Max Stafford-Clark

NICK HERN BOOKS
London
www.nickhernbooks.co.uk

A Nick Hern Book

DRAMA GAMES
FOR CLASSROOMS AND WORKSHOPS

Reprinted 2009, 2010, 2011, 2012, 2013,
2014, 2015, 2016, 2017

First published in Great Britain in 2009
by Nick Hern Books Limited
The Glasshouse, 49a Goldhawk Road,
London W12 8QP

Cover designed by www.energydesignstudio.com
Typeset by Nick Hern Books, London
Printed and bound in Great Britain by
Ashford Colour Press, Gosport, Hampshire

A CIP catalogue record for this book
is available from the British Library

ISBN 978 1 84842 010 6

For James, with love

FOREWORD

I know Jessica Swale as a conscientious, talented and intelligent, young director. She was my assistant on *The Overwhelming*, JT Rogers' fine play that opened at the National Theatre in a National/Out of Joint co-production in early 2006. She was a warm, inventive and positive presence in the rehearsal room. The actors loved her. I was even more impressed when she started her own theatre company, Red Handed, shortly afterwards. It requires tenacity, vision and courage to start your own theatre company in these times.

In this book, she has written an extraordinarily helpful compendium and guide to drama games that will be a valuable help to directors, teachers and workshop leaders.

One of the strange anomalies of theatre is that 'play', 'enjoyment' and indeed 'childishness' is such an essential part of the rehearsal room, but we have to plan and work hard to attain it. The director must also then apply it. I recall clearly as a young director observing the rehearsals of a director who was slightly my senior. Her rehearsals were exuberant, inventive and original. But when I saw the eventual production that emerged from these rehearsals it contained very little of these qualities. We must structure and work for invention and spontaneity but we must then return to the text and apply it. The liveliness of the rehearsal room must inform the text.

Jessica's book makes no claim to be either comprehensive or original. The games she lists are a stimulus to further invention and imagination: invent your own games. Her games have been pinched from everywhere. I recognised several of mine in there and in return I started making a list of games that I would pinch. I stopped when the list reached over twenty, and resolved to make the book a permanent assistant.

If you can't get to a workshop run by Jessica Swale then invite her to your next party, whether it is for kids or adults. She will be of hilarious value!

Max Stafford-Clark

CONTENTS

Part Five – TEAMWORK

Part Six – TRUST

Part Seven – CHARACTER
Introducing Characterisation

Character Development

Part Eight – STORYTELLING

INTRODUCTION

Why Play?

*To play needs much work. But when we experience
the work as play, then it is not work any more.
A play is play.* Peter Brook

The concept of 'play' has been a foundation of
theatrical tradition for many years, since
Stanislavsky and his contemporaries incorporated
exercises into rehearsals. Games are used in the
pursuit of the soul of a character, to explore the
'world of the play' and to create dynamic
relationships on stage. When used effectively,
games can provide unparalleled opportunities for
exploration and discovery. Whether working in a
theatre company or in a school, in youth theatre or
in outreach, they form an essential part of every
modern practitioner's toolkit.

The enduring popularity of drama games can be
explained by the expansive range of skills that they
develop in the participants. To actors, these
exercises offer a lively means of exploring emotion,
situation and character. For students, they provide
an imaginative platform from which to jump, and in
the community they offer a safe means of
overcoming inhibitions and building relationships.
Games can promote teamwork, spontaneity,
confidence, trust and creativity, and many of them
can be easily adapted to suit a range of workshop
objectives. But how do you choose which to use?
Where do you start and what are the challenges?

So often games are used as time-fillers by
uninspired drama teachers who haven't planned
anything more structured to do. I remember the
recurring feeling of disheartenment as a theatre-
obsessed teenager, when, after playing *Stuck in the*

Mud for half an hour, the drama teacher would utter the dreaded phrase, 'We've got one hour left so… go off and make up a play.' Such unstructured sessions may occasionally provide creative opportunities by accident, but they can hardly be classed as stimulating. Creating dynamic drama workshops is not difficult, it just requires forethought. Games must be carefully selected; each exercise should filter into the wider objectives of the lesson like a tributary into a river. A good facilitator uses games like bricks to build towards a specific outcome. Choose the wrong bricks, and the lesson crumbles.

Distinctions Between Drama and Theatre

Drama games can be as useful in a social or educational context as they are in the theatre. The activities in this book work equally well in both scenarios. Whilst, as a director, I have used many of these games in rehearsal, sometimes their most rewarding use has been in the classroom, where young and inexperienced students have surprised themselves with their own imaginative capacity.

The games arise from a variety of sources. Some have roots in traditional children's games. However, it is vital to note that playground games and drama activities are not one and the same. Some forms of traditional play promote competitiveness and superiority. In contrast, whilst there is often room for individuality in drama, its primary aim is to develop collaboration as a form of creative learning. Drama is, in a sense, an extension of play, refining certain aspects of natural play whilst discouraging elements that are counterproductive in a creative environment, like egoism.

Positive skill-building is the foundation of 'drama' as an activity. This, in turn, is an ideal starting point for theatre-making. However, whether you want to extend your drama workshop towards the goal of performance is entirely your choice. Whilst theatre is a medium of performance created for the benefit of an audience, drama exists for the sake of its own participants. It is an active subject that uses theatrical values as a basis for creative engagement. This is a critical distinction to be made by those of us who work both as directors and workshop facilitators – it is all too easy to be unfair and demand great performances from workshop participants who simply want to 'take part' and gain social skills.

The Content of Your Workshop

The correct approach to workshop-leading has been a topic of debate for many years. Whether called a 'workshop leader', 'director', 'teacher', 'difficultator', 'overseer' or 'side-coach', the role of the drama facilitator is undeniably complex. As Joan Littlewood commented, 'Chaos has to be very well organised.'

A well-run drama session can offer a creative springboard, a chance to escape into an imaginative realm, a means of making something visceral and exciting which, whilst temporal, is shared in that moment by the participants in the room. This is the joy of facilitating.

Whatever the educational goals of a workshop, be they theatrical, creative, social or academic, there are two essential aspects of a successful session:

1. The participants ought to feel that something has been achieved; they have created something, learned fresh concepts, gained skills or developed new bonds.

2. There must always be a sense of vitality and excitement. It is all too easy to lose sight of this in a quest to provide an informative experience.

You will undoubtedly find that, in an entertaining workshop, the students will absorb the material with ease. This explains why drama is now being used so frequently across the curriculum, and why issue-based theatre workshops are so popular in schools. As a young drama teacher, I was asked to teach Religious Studies in my free periods. I was hesitant to accept at first; however, I soon began to enjoy the challenge as I used drama to enliven the lessons. At the end of the year, my greatest concern was that other staff would think my students had cheated when final exam results revealed that every one scored over ninety per cent. But it was simply the use of drama as a kinaesthetic learning tool that helped them absorb the material so thoroughly – the story of John the Baptist as told on 'J the B TV' by a dynamic rapping trio certainly ensured every member of the class knew the tale inside out!

It is important to remember that there are no wrong answers in drama, and participants should not be discouraged for creating a 'bad scene'. Of course, you can set parameters in order to improve technique, if your goals are theatrical, but always try and encourage participants to make improvements in a positive manner. 'That was really dramatic, now try and turn to us a little more so that we don't miss any of the exciting dialogue' is far more encouraging than 'Never have your backs to us when you are talking!'

In rehearsal, directors will be sure to find that the joy of playing often gives rise to creativity. I have often found the most original work with my theatre company, Red Handed, has sprung from game-filled rehearsals that allow the actors to experiment imaginatively with the text. Further, game-playing as a company allows a cooperative, creative spirit to develop that encourages greater collaboration. Whilst working with Max Stafford-Clark, I quickly learnt the benefit of using games throughout the rehearsal process to encourage actors to fully explore their roles. In early rehearsals he uses improvisation games to explore context and plot, then later exercises delve into the specifics of characterisation and objectives. His selective use of games encourages actors to work towards an incredible level of detail, that is electricfying in performance.

Safety and Welfare

The facilitator has certain basic responsibilities, regardless of the particular circumstances of their workshop. Hazard awareness must always be a primary concern. Always ensure that you arrive early enough to check the room for potential risks, and plan your workshop carefully according to the size of the space available. Think ahead about activities that include an element of risk. Trust exercises in particular, like *Falling Trees* (Game 59) or *Leap of Faith* (Game 58), ought to be used only when you know the participants well enough to trust them to undertake the exercises sensibly.

The facilitator must also take responsibility for the welfare of the participants. Non-actors will often be nervous about the level of public exposure they might be subject to. Confidence-building games are an ideal tool to encourage such hesitant participants. Attempt to structure each workshop so that participants work as a group before progressing to more demanding, creative activities in smaller teams or pairs. This allows the players to feel comfortable with each other before being put 'in the spotlight'. A responsible facilitator will guide and encourage each participant through the creative process and watch carefully to ensure every individual is coping with the demands of the exercises.

The facilitator also has to be responsible for the emotional demands of the workshop, as acting so often entails the exploration of personal feelings. As theatre is a reflection of life, be aware that there can be participants who will have been affected by subjects in the drama. In asking the participants to share emotionally within the group, you are asking them to expose themselves in a manner that is unusual outside the theatre. In this context, the facilitator must be a supportive, caring coercer. Ensure you choose your activities carefully, in order to work at a level of emotional exploration appropriate for your group. You must remain aware that the process of making theatre is also about how to live, and about the sharing of values and ideals that should inform every rehearsal.

Bringing the Text to Life

The process of bringing the text to life – of drawing out the characters from the words – can often be challenging. Sometimes it is tempting to follow an intellectual approach, methodically deconstructing the text. However, this can deaden the work and result in actors becoming detached. Stanislavsky portentously warns that:

> Intellectual analysis, if undertaken by itself and for its own sake, is harmful because its mathematical, dry qualities tend to chill an impulse of artistic élan and creative enthusiasm.

He suggests an artistic approach, as, 'If the result of scholarly analysis is thought, the result of artistic analysis is feeling.' But how does one attempt artistic analysis? Surely it must be an imaginative approach, a playful approach, without the binds of academic deconstruction. Certainly, games provide one of the greatest tools for exploring the text creatively. Several games in this book specifically provide methods for investigating the spoken word (see Part Seven: Character). Through investigating specific language choices, objectives and interpretation, the actors will undoubtedly find detail and intrigue in the text that may have previously gone unnoticed.

How to Use This Book

This book is designed as a dip-in, flick-through, quick-fire resource book that you can sling into your bag and pull out at an opportune moment. However, the material here is also suitable for planning entire workshops from start to finish. The book is divided into sections that enable you to see the specific focus of each game easily, allowing you to plan where it might be best suited in a workshop – handy warm-up games to start off, followed by skills tasks, extended exercises, and finally, cool-downs, in order to ensure the participants have time to reflect and recover from their active drama sessions!

After the summary of 'How to Play', you will often find suggestions for 'Variations and Extensions'. The 'Variations' provide engaging alternatives to usual play, to allow you to use the game again in a different session with a new slant to capture the players' imaginations. The 'Extensions' show ways to develop the games, to explore skills in more depth, to pursue ideas further in the development of scenarios, to to delve into historical or theatrical concepts that relate closely to the games, thereby extending players' intellectual and physical skills. Many relate directly to the National Curriculum, for leaders using the games for GCSE or A-level groups.

Whilst the book is divided into sections according to the primary focus of each game, almost every game teaches multiple skills and could fit into a number of categories. For this reason, at the bottom of each page you will find a panel summarising the key aptitudes tested by the game. You will also find a suggested minimum age of the players. The age guide is meant merely as a handy tool for planning, to suggest games that are particularly suitable for younger players. It is by no means intended to exclude others. Having used most of these games with both actors and students, I have found that many assumed 'children's games' can yield imaginative, and often hilarious, results when played with adults. One of the benefits of creative games is that many can be played at different levels according to the players. Games like *Freeze!* (Game 89) and *Word Wizard* (Game 84) are particular examples, and I have often had to insist vehemently that it was time to move on when adult actors simply wanted to go on playing *King of the Jungle* (Game 35)!

In the panel following each game, alongside the age recommendation and skills, you will find a suggestion of the group size. This is a rough estimation but some games work less well – or would even be dangerous – with an inappropriate number of players: *Leap of Faith* (Game 58) and *Friendly Follower* (Game 57), for example.

You will also find a suggested time period for each game, which will help you to plan the content of a workshop carefully. The time period suggested is the actual playing time, so if you are using an activity for the first time, be sure to add extra time for explaining the rules and having a practice round. I'm sure you will often find that an exercise yields interesting developments; so often, the best workshops are those that naturally develop in an unexpected direction as a consequence of participants' spontaneity and creativity. Do ensure, for this reason, that you do not try to cram in too many activities, to avoid frustration and to allow time to pursue imaginative discoveries.

You will also find an indication of any 'additional requirements' in the panel at the foot of each page, which indicates any factors that need to be prepared in advance; the use of props, for instance, or the provision of music.

There are many factors to take into account when planning a workshop, and so you will find a cross-reference index at the back of this book. This will allow you to select games using other useful categories, such as the key skills developed, group size (games for pairs, solos, etc.), games that require preparation, games for advanced players, and games that initiate further creative opportunities.

Every game in this book has been tried and tested, adapted, reformed and reused. Some games are favourites with young children, others with foreign students and others with professional actors; one thing is for sure – many of these games can be equally creative when played with five or fifty-year-olds! The games come from all manner of sources, and I have collected and edited them over the years. I apologise if any appear to be 'other people's games', but games, like the plots of plays, are continually shared, borrowed, adapted and recycled. I have attempted to collect as wide a range as possible and not to replicate, and you will no doubt recognise some games under different titles. I have tried to give credit where credit is due, but most are from the melting pot of resources that is shared in modern practice.

The Power of Play

Having worked as a teacher, director and educator, I have used these games in a host of contrasting scenarios. I shall give just one example of the potency of games to yield benefits; it is an example that truly reflects their capacity to initiate creativity, theatricality, personal skills and community.

In 2008 I was invited to work as a theatre director for Youth Bridge Global, a non-governmental organisation founded by Professor Andrew Garrod, that uses theatre in the developing world as a vehicle for imparting skills and bridging social gaps. I travelled to the Marshall Islands, a tiny developing nation in the North West Pacific Ocean, tasked with the challenge of directing a bilingual version of *The Comedy of Errors* in ten weeks, with a group of the islands' high-school students. On arrival I was shocked by the limitations of their English-language skills, and, not being a natural linguist, began to sweat profusely at the daunting challenge of creating a theatre production – a Shakespeare production at that – without a shared vocabulary!

Many of the cast had no previous experience of drama as there is no local theatrical tradition on the islands. Even more surprising was the lack of texts available to read, in either in English or Marshallese, so the students' literary skills were extremely limited. This was surely going to be a test of the power of drama, and workshop games specifically, to bridge the vast gap between the team of tutors and the actors. Daily rehearsals would soon reveal whether workshops could genuinely make an impact amongst disenfranchised youth. The islands suffer from an array of social problems, mainly brought about through poverty and reliance on foreign aid. Today, aid from the US accounts for over sixty per cent of the country's GDP, making the Marshall Islands the most foreign-aid dependent nation in the world.

Living in a community with few openings for self-improvement, the young people were hungry for this opportunity to develop skills and ultimately improve employability. Over the following ten weeks, the benefits of using exercises daily with the cast became almost tangible. With a limited shared vocabulary, the language of drama – action, movement, expression, sound – became our means of communication. Easy warm-up games that necessitated little grasp of English (*Mexican Clap*, Game 37, for instance) immediately gave us some common ground. The simple aim of achieving a shared goal transcended any language barriers and soon the kids were all whooping and laughing as they broke their own time record. As sessions progressed we introduced more complex games (*Star Wars*, Game 54, for instance) in which they began to work cohesively as a team… and learn a little more about Western culture! By week four, they had mastered the art of *Freeze!* (Game 89), arriving at some stunning improvisation scenarios, having built confidence over the previous weeks with imaginative exercises like *Super Chair* (Game 80). Working in this manner, slowly increasing the complexity of the tasks, the students' skills improved steadily. Further, their English vocabulary was expanding dramatically; much more quickly, I am ashamed to say, than my Marshallese.

Their final performances exceeded all my expectations and remain a testament to the power of drama to build confidence and community. The incredible transformation of the nervous, script-shy auditionees to the exuberant cast in performance is due mainly, I am sure, to the playful work we undertook together in rehearsal. Through working closely as a company, making discoveries together, we were able to share our experiences and create an event in which we had all invested. Over the final few nights, word of the cast's success spread quickly and well over a thousand local people turned out, alongside the islands' President and many other notable local dignitaries.

Whilst I am incredibly proud of their performances, the greatest outcome is that the cast are now planning an independent production for next year. This will be the first ever Marshallese-produced play, to my knowledge. They now feel empowered to step beyond our outsider-led project, having found the skills and confidence necessary to 'go it alone'. This, surely, is the ultimate goal of every drama facilitator; to be able to step back and confidently say, 'Now you don't need me any more.' The games this group played over the ten weeks promoted confidence, trust, team-building and empowerment, always underscored with a sense of fun. I am convinced that our communal game-playing is responsible for this most gratifying result, and I urge you to use these exercises positively to encourage your actors, whether they are professionals, students, members of the community – or Pacific Islanders.

I hope you enjoy playing these games as much as I do.

Jessica Swale

ACKNOWLEDGEMENTS

I feel privileged to have shared in the plethora of activities that characterise contemporary drama and theatre practice. These provide the foundations for this book.

My own work and philosophy owes a great deal to Max Stafford-Clark, an inspiring director whose use of inventive games in rehearsal encourages a level of detail that is magnetising in performance. The writings of Augusto Boal, Peter Brook and Mike Alfreds continually reinforce my belief in the importance of 'play' in making plays. In education, Catherine Saker and Ron Price are responsible for proving to me how much fun a drama lesson could, and should, be. Further, I am indebted to Professor Andrew Garrod, founder of Youth Bridge Global, for the opportunity to experience drama's remarkable capacity as a development tool.

A constant source of inspiration and inventors of many games, my parents sowed a playful seed in my imagination which I am ever grateful for. Alongside them, this book would not have been possible without the support of my dear friends Kristin, Vinny and Lindsey, who inspired me to keep on writing, despite the tropical heat and many distractions of the Marshall Islands!

Jo Kennedy, my ever-enthusiastic Creative Producer at Red Handed has been an invaluable source of support and advice. I am also indebted to Nick Hern and Matt Applewhite, whose generosity and wholehearted belief in this project has made the writing of this book a real pleasure.

Finally, I would not have written a word without the inspiration of the actors and students who turn up for my rehearsals and classes, giving themselves utterly, and continually surprising me with their imaginative capacity. To all of you, thank you.

PART ONE

WARM-UP

Body

Rubber Chicken!

A fast-paced, team-building warm-up game that gets a group going quickly.

How to Play

Ask the players to stand in a circle. Explain that you are all going to shake your right hands up in the air eight times, whilst counting loudly and quickly – '8, 7, 6, 5, 4, 3, 2, 1!' Then you are going to repeat this with your left hand, then right leg, then left leg. The counting needs to be fast and loud, and the shaking needs to be vigorous and energetic. As soon as you have done all four limbs from 8 to 1, repeat the shaking and counting from 7 to 1, then 6 to 1, and continue until you finally shake each limb once, counting, '1, 1, 1, 1!' Then everyone shouts 'Rubber chicken!' and shakes their whole body like a rubber chicken!

The Aim of the Game

The aim is for the whole group to complete the routine vigorously and enthusiastically as a team. The game also builds their energy levels and gets them moving.

You can easily replace the phrase 'rubber chicken' with a word that means something to your group, the name of the play you are rehearsing, or your theatre company or school, to give a feeling of group solidarity and positive energy!

Players	Age	Time	Skills
Any number	6+	3	Movement, Teamwork, Energy

Greyhound Race

A quick circle game that encourages everyone to get moving and get involved by mimicking a sports crowd, and the sport, simultaneously.

How to Play

Ask the players to stand in a circle. Explain that they are at the greyhound races and, to everyone's excitement, the greyhound is going to race around the track right under our feet! When you say 'Go!', the dog will be let out and will run as fast as it can in the designated direction (to your left or right). As the imaginary dog passes under your feet, you must jump as high as possible to let it past. You must watch as it whizzes round the circle, and the louder you cheer, the faster it will go!

On your shout ('Go!'), each of the players then jumps up in the air in turn, as quickly as possible, to allow the greyhound to pass underneath them. Give a running commentary as 'the sports commentator' to enliven the game, and to help the players imagine the dog as it is running past:

> *He's coming round the final bend, he seems to be slowing down, maybe if we cheer louder he'll run even faster, look at the sweat pouring off him, he's almost there, a little bit faster... and he's done it!!*

When playing with older groups you can pass the 'commentator' role to a responsible player. Once the greyhound has done several rounds, you can announce that it has won.

The Aim of the Game

The aim is for the players to work as a team to create the idea of the moving greyhound. Everyone needs to participate and jump up – if one person doesn't jump, the whole race will slow down. By encouraging cheering you can also stretch the players' imaginative skills and increase the feeling of teamwork, as they encourage each other to jump quicker to help the greyhound win!

Players	Age	Time	Skills
10+	6+	5	*Energy, Teamwork, Coordination*

MTV Cameraman

A hilarious physical warm-up game, in which players use body parts as a pop-music video camera.

How to Play

Ask the players to find a space. They must imagine that they are the newest hot-shot film-maker, the guy (or girl) behind the latest music videos. They are now going to shoot their best pop video yet... using a part of their body.

On the sole of their left foot there is an imaginary video camera. Balancing on their other foot, they can now begin to make the film. In order to create a cool video, they need to move their foot through every angle, zoom in on interesting people and objects, whilst moving their 'camera' in time to the imaginary music. Encourage them to video the whole room; behind them, in front of them, the ceiling, and the floor. The wilder the film, the better! Then move onto the right foot, and any other body parts you choose.

The Aim of the Game

Primarily the aim is to physically warm up the players by encouraging them to manipulate their bodies in every direction. It also encourages an awareness of rhythm and demands imaginative thinking.

Variations and Extensions

This game can easily be played with imaginary music, but you could use a CD if you wish. You can also vary the music style each time you begin with a new body part, to encourage them to explore various musical forms; e.g. a slow, lyrical video as opposed to a flashy disco-mix. This also encourages players to think about emotions and genres.

+ Recorded music (optional)			
Players	**Age**	**Time**	**Skills**
Any number	6+	5	Movement, Imagination, Improvisation, Rhythm

Super Shake

An extremely simple but amusing warm-up game, in which players pass 'the shakes' to each other.

How to Play

Ask the players to stand in a circle. Explain that you have the dreaded disease 'The Shakes', and it is highly contagious!

You begin the game by shaking a body part; for instance, your left hand. The more shocked you act that you have caught the shakes, the better! The shakes become extremely vigorous, and the only way of getting rid of them is to 'throw' them to another player across the circle, by physically shaking at them.

They must catch the shakes in the same body part, and then transfer it to another part of their body. They then 'throw' the new shake to someone else, and thus the game continues.

The Aim of the Game

The game encourages teamwork and physical confidence – the more you shake, and the more fearful you are of the shakes, the funnier the game! Encourage older players to be inventive with the body parts they choose; it is a hilarious sight to see people catching the shakes in the knee, the eye or even the tongue!

WARM-UP

Players	Age	Time	Skills
4+	6+	5	Movement, Confidence, Focus

Mirror, Mirror...

A physical game that involves passing movements around the ring; a 'bodily version' of Chinese Whispers.

How to Play

Ask the players to stand in a circle. You begin by doing a simple movement (e.g. jump and point) towards the person on your right, let's call her Claire. Claire must then do exactly the same movement back at you, before turning and repeating it to the person on her right, Becky. Becky then copies Claire's movement back to her, before passing it on to her right-hand neighbour, Natalie, and the game continues.

The idea is to pass the exact movement around the whole circle. However, if anything changes – e.g. if someone laughs halfway through, or gets the movement slightly wrong – the next person must copy what they saw, not the initial movement. Inevitably, the movement that comes back around to you at the end of the circle is likely to be very different from the one you initiated, and can often provoke hysterics amongst the players!

When the group has become adept at passing the movement round, you can introduce a second movement, and pass it in the other direction around the circle. The point at which the two movements swap places is a great source of amusement! You can add more movements to make the game more challenging.

The Aim of the Game

The game encourages physical alertness, concentration, and stresses the importance of observation skills for actors.

Variations and Extensions

Try adding sound to each movement to create a greater challenge for older or experienced players.

Players	Age	Time	Skills
8+	**8+**	**5**	*Energy, Teamwork, Coordination*

Yes, Let's!

Perhaps the most positive of all drama games, an encouraging, energetic and enthusiastic team game involving improvisation. In this game, anything goes!

How to Play

Ask the group to spread out and find a space. During the game, players offer suggestions for spontaneous activities. Each suggestion must begin with 'I know, let's...' Suggestions can be as simple or as wacky as you like.

Take the lead by making the first suggestion; e.g. 'I know, let's... snorkel!' or 'Let's go on an adventure!' or 'Let's wriggle around on the floor!' All the players then energetically reply 'Yes, let's!' and then perform or mime that activity.

Players then make suggestions as and when they have an idea. Any player can make an 'I know, let's...' suggestion at any time, and the more creative the ideas are, the better. Do encourage every player to offer ideas, even if they are simple ('skip', 'walk') and try and keep the momentum of the suggestions coming so as not to lose energy.

The Aim of the Game

This is an incredibly positive and empowering game that encourages every player to get involved, both in the activities and in the suggestions.

Variations and Extensions

With older players, encourage them to make open-ended suggestions that could be taken in a number of contexts. For instance, 'Let's be', when vocalised, often results in a few people standing and contemplating, simply 'be-ing', and others buzzing around the room like a bee. This can be a very interesting and thoughtful activity and has even been used as a performance in its own right!

Players	Age	Time	Skills
4+	8+	10	*Energy, Imagination, Dynamism*

The Incredible Itch

A physical game that gets people moving, reacting, itching and exaggerating with a vengeance! A fast and funny game for all ages.

How to Play

Ask the players to find a space. Explain that you have some bad news – you have heard a rumour that 'the itching plague' is coming! When you get the plague, dreadful things begin to happen to you. At stage one, you think you have a little itch, but by stage ten you are dead! During the game, the players have to imagine that they have caught the plague and use their bodies in the most interesting and dramatic ways to stop themselves from itching.

Begin the game by announcing that 'The plague has arrived!' Then begin slowly counting from 1 to 10. As the numbers get higher, the players get itchier and itchier. They begin by imagining they have a slight tickle, then the itch becomes stronger, slowly spreading from one or two places on their bodies until their whole bodies are itching like crazy! At this stage, they have to wriggle and writhe on the floor or against a wall to control the itchiness, until, when you get to 10, the plague overpowers them and they drop down dead!

Whilst the theme sounds a little morbid, this is a hugely popular game in my classes, particularly amongst younger classes and boys, who find it hilarious!

The Aim of the Game

The game encourages a great deal of movement so it is an excellent warm-up. Perhaps the game's best quality, however, is its emphasis on pacing. As the numbers increase, the focus on the slow development of the itching plague clearly links into the importance of building pace and momentum in drama. Link this to the concept of building up emotion, tension or dynamics in a scene or a play.

Variations and Extensions

You can try a more detailed version of this game with older players, in order to encourage specificity and mime skills. 'The itching plague' can evolve into a much more elaborate disease, by giving specific instructions for each number.

For instance:

1. Slight tickle
2. Itchy extremities
3. The itch spreads
4. Cold sweats
5. Hot flushes
6. Boils begin to develop and pop
7. Nausea
8. Convulsions
9. Hysteria
10. Death

This is a hilarious variation and is an excellent tool for mime work when played silently, or for Commedia dell'Arte workshops if played with sound.

You can also substitute the itching plague for an alternative physical or emotional idea. Try building happiness or fear from 1 to 10 (although, be warned, the latter can get a little loud!). You can add a scenario to make the game more dramatic, for instance, waiting in line for an injection. Every number means you move one step closer to the front of the queue! Allow emotion to build up using the face, voice and body.

Players	Age	Time	Skills
Any number	6+	10	Movement, Confidence, Imagination, Pacing

Daily-Routine Disco

An imaginative and hilarious mime game that asks players to create exaggerated dances from daily routines.

How to Play

Ask the players to find a space. Then ask them to pick a standard daily routine, and to mime it in as much detail as possible. They must do this on their own and avoid watching other players. Suitable routines include 'getting-up' rituals like having a shave, washing hair, brushing teeth or taking a shower, or regular activities such as driving a car, baking a cake, writing a letter, cleaning the house.

Explain that you are going to count slowly from 1 to 10. Each time you say a number, the players must enlarge and exaggerate their actions by ten per cent. Facial expressions, gestures, rhythms and small body movements must all grow, until they reach epic proportions. The aim is for the simple, realistic mime to become a melodramatic, exaggerated dance. Encourage them to use the routine's rhythms to give them a beat for the dance. By 10, the original routine should barely be recognisable, and they should be using their entire bodies in their 'daily-routine dance'.

After counting from 1 to 10 and ensuring all of their dances are big and bold, ask them to line up facing the playing space. Choose one person to be 'up' and ask them to perform their daily-routine dance. The others have to watch carefully, trying to identify what the original activity might have been. If they think they know, they must go and join in the dance on stage. Before long you will have a daily-routine disco, where a group of players are all dancing the routine together. At a certain point, stop them, and ask the participating players to identify what they thought the original activity was, one by one. When they have all guessed, ask the original player to reveal their initial routine. You will sometimes be surprised by the answers!

Then ask for another volunteer to perform their dance, and repeat the exercise.

The Aim of the Game

The game promotes mime skills and imagination, confidence and energy. The aim is to encourage everyone to explore melodrama, and to understand how movement and dance can be generated from the simplest of actions.

Variations and Extensions

You do not have to limit your discos to the bounds of daily routines. For extra amusement you might like to throw in a location as a starting point; for instance, 'At the zoo' or 'On holiday'. The routines the players choose should be rooted in this scenario; e.g. feeding the penguins, cleaning out the elephants, working in pets' corner. This can be particularly useful for exploring a scenario playfully during devising projects.

Players	Age	Time	Skills
Any number	8+	10	Mime, Confidence, Movement, Imagination

Cat and Mouse

A fast-paced warm-up game, in which players have to escape from the cat by joining up with other players.

How to Play

Choose a player to be 'the cat' and another to be 'the mouse'. Everyone else must get into pairs and find a space in the room, linking arms with their partner. The pairs are not allowed to move from their spot.

The cat's aim is to catch the mouse. In order to escape, the mouse runs around the room. If he hooks on to one of the players in a pair by linking arms with them, the player on the other end has to let go and becomes the mouse. If the mouse is caught, then cat becomes mouse, and mouse becomes cat, so the chase changes direction.

The Aim of the Game

This is a very simple but exhilarating warm-up game. The aim is to loosen the players up physically, as the game demands speed and agility. It also promotes awareness skills because players are never safe, there is the chance that they could become the mouse at any moment!

Variations and Extensions

Another version of this game is *Shadows*. The aims are the same, but it is a little harder and therefore better for older players. Everyone spreads out around the room and stands still, facing the middle of the room. Allocate a runner and a chaser. The runner must try and escape from the chaser. The runner can choose to swap out at any time, by standing directly in front of one of the other stationary players. At this point the player behind them (their shadow) becomes the runner. If the chaser catches the runner, they swap roles and the chase changes direction. This is a fast-paced and exhilarating game that always keeps players on their toes.

Players	Age	Time	Skills
8+	8+	10	*Pacing, Focus, Awareness*

Face

Pass the Face

A simple but hilarious circle game that warms up the face and encourages confidence.

How to Play

Ask the players to stand in a circle. In this game you must 'pass the face' around the circle, but each time someone new receives it, they transform it into another face.

You begin the exercise by pulling a funny face. Then turn in slow motion to your right-hand neighbour, let's call her Katie, continuing to pull the face. Katie must mirror you exactly, in equally slow motion. Holding that facial expression, she then turns to her right-hand neighbour, Jack. As she turns past the middle of the circle, she slowly transforms your funny face into a different expression. Jack must then mirror Katie's face, then turns to the next person, changing the expression again, and the game continues.

You can easily 'theme' each round of the circle with an emotion, in order to explore all the facial expressions we associate with a specific feeling. Each person must find a new facial expression to express a quality of the chosen emotion, so the game gets progressively harder as you get further round the circle. There is a surprising amount of scope within this exercise; even in large groups players manage to find new possibilities. It can also act as an effective starting point for characterisation exercises.

The Aim of the Game

The aim is to encourage the group to be as dynamic and inventive as possible in their face-pulling, and in doing so, to discover a range of varied characters. Each face should be totally different from the last. By using slow motion you will encourage a higher degree of focus amongst the players. It is also an effective facial warm-up. Try speeding it up to super-speed in order to add energy and hilarity!

Variations and Extensions

This game is a great starting point for exploring the links between facial expressions and emotion. Follow the game with a discussion in which you ask the group to identify how the regions of the face reveal emotions. Talk though each facial feature and work through the various feelings suggested by its varied positions. For instance, encourage them all to raise, lower, angle and furrow their eyebrows. What does an audience think when they see a character using each of these expressions? This is a good grounding for subsequent detailed work on characterisation.

You can also adapt this game to encourage exploration of specific characters or character types. When exploring a play, for instance, choose a character and ask the players to reveal all the faces of that individual. This is particularly engaging for Shakespeare workshops, in which characters like Macbeth present such a vast and complex range of emotions.

Players	Age	Time	Skills
4+	6+	5	Movement, Confidence, Imagination, Character

Ooey, Gooey, Chewy Gum

A vocal and facial warm-up game, in which players pass the ever-changing gum around the circle.

How to Play

Ask the players to stand in a circle. Explain to them that you have been lucky enough to get hold of a very special delicious delight, the 'Ooey, Gooey, Chewy Gum'. Everyone in the world would love to try this gum. Unlike conventional gum which loses flavour, the more you chew, the stronger the flavour becomes! You have generously decided to share your last piece of Ooey, Gooey, Chewy Gum with the group. But, be warned: it is an acquired taste – to some people it will taste delicious, but others will find it disgusting!

Begin by putting the imaginary chewing gum in your mouth. Chew it slowly, making appropriate gum-chewing sound effects (this is essential to the game's value as a vocal warm-up), giving your mouth and lips a good workout. Then mime taking the gum out of your mouth, and pass it on to the next player… this action in itself is likely to get a reaction from the group!

Remind them that the gum will taste delicious to some and vile to others, so as they begin to chew, we should see and hear their reaction to the taste. The taste of the gum gets stronger the more it is chewed, so as it progresses around the circle, reactions should get more and more exaggerated, until the final person is almost rolling on the ground, either in delirious joy or absolute repulsion!

Encourage the players to use their voices, faces and, eventually, whole bodies, in their reactions to the taste of the gum.

The Aim of the Game

The aim of the game is primarily to warm the actors' faces up. However, this is also a good exercise for exploring melodrama and exaggeration.

Players	Age	Time	Skills
Any number	**6+**	**5**	*Imagination, Voice, Confidence*

Funny Face

Possibly the simplest drama game ever invented, but one of the most endearing, in which the actors explore their facial flexibility to music.

How to Play

Divide the group in two. Ask half of the group to be the 'experimenters' and find a space to sit comfortably on the floor, facing the audience (the other half of the group).

Choose a piece of music. Something slow and relaxed works ideally; e.g. Billie Holliday or Ella Fitzgerald. The experimenters can then begin. They have the entire length of the song to experiment with their facial flexibility. They should explore the movement of their eyes, nose, mouth, as if they were pulling faces at themselves in a mirror. The more focused they are, the more they will find out about their own faces, and the more characters they will undoubtedly discover. Emphasise that their aim is to experiment with their own faces, rather than to perform for the audience's benefit.

The audience will no doubt watch with great amusement, but encourage them to be respectful and quiet. Once the song is over, ask the audience what they found interesting. Then ask the two groups to swap over. You may wish to use a different piece of music for the second group.

The Aim of the Game

The aim is simple; to allow individuals to fully explore the possibilities of their facial expressiveness. It also encourages good audience skills from the watching players.

+ Recorded music			
Players	**Age**	**Time**	**Skills**
Any number	6+	10	Imagination, Focus, Character

Voice

Boom-chicka-boom!

A fun vocal warm-up that involves repeating responses in a range of styles.

How to Play

This is a simple call and response game that gets the group moving, singing and rocking. Ask the group to stand in a circle and to repeat each line after you. They should also move to the rhythm as much as possible. Every time you get to the end of the rhyme, you are going to give them a new style to perform in, so they need to be ready to improvise!

YOU: I say a boom –

THEM: I say a boom –

YOU: I say a boom-chicka –

THEM: I say a boom-chicka –

YOU: I say a boom-chicka-boom –

THEM: I say a boom-chicka-boom –

YOU: I say a boom-chicka-boom –

THEM: I say a boom-chicka-boom –

YOU: I say a boom-chicka-rocka-chicka-rocka-chicka-boom –

THEM: I say a boom-chicka-rocka-chicka-rocka-chicka-boom –

YOU: Oh yeah!

THEM: Oh yeah!

YOU: That's right!

THEM: That's right!

YOU: One more time!

THEM: One more time!

YOU: In … style.

THEM: … style.

In the final line, insert a new style of your choice. Suggestions that work well include DJ style, opera style, Wild West style, puppet style, speedy style, slow-mo style, holy style, sexy style, musical style, elderly style, playground style. In fact, anything goes!

The Aim of the Game

The aim is to get the group working together in an energetic, creative and rhythmic manner.

Variations and Extensions

With younger players, you might like to give an emotion rather than a style. This is a simple way of encouraging them to think about portraying feelings using voice and body language. With older participants, you might like to pass the 'leader' role around the circle, so that each person gets the chance to suggest a style and to lead.

A further extension, to allow greater creativity amongst older players, is to ask them to try the same exercise using lines from a play. Choose a short passage that they know off by heart, ask the rest of the group to create a basic rhythm by clapping in time, and get them to have a go. When they have performed it in one style, throw in another. This is a challenging yet engaging exercise, and works particularly well with musical students.

WARM-UP

Players	Age	Time	Skills
Any number	8+	10	Improvisation, Rhythm, Teamwork

WARM-UP

The Ultimate Tongue-Twisting Challenge

A selection of vocal warm-ups to get the mouth muscles working.

How to Play

Tongue twisters are a useful tool for the drama coach, as they are a fun activity for warming up the vocal muscles and teaching articulation. They can be used in a number of ways. I like the group to perform them super slowly at first in order to get their mouths around each of the syllables. As an initial activity, ask them to imagine they are on slow-motion playback as they speak each line, exaggerating each word, and trying to use every facial muscle to add interesting dynamics.

Here are some tongue twisters that explore a range of varied sounds. You may wish simply to learn them as a group and see how fast you can perform them. Alternatively you can use them as a round, or add movements.

The Tooting Tudor
　　A Tudor who tooted a flute
　　Tried to tutor two tooters to toot.
　　Said the two to their tutor,
　　'Is it harder to toot
　　Or to tutor two tooters to toot?'

Give Me the Gift
　　Give me the gift of a grip-top sock,
　　A dip-drape, shipshape, tip-top sock,
　　Not your silly, slapstick, slip-slop sock,
　　But a plastic, elastic grip-top sock!

What a To-Do!
　　What a to-do, to die, today at a minute or
　　　　two to two,
　　A thing distinctly hard to say, but a harder
　　　　thing to do,
　　For they'll beat a tattoo at two today, a rat-
　　　　a-tat-tat at two,
　　And the dragon will come when he hears
　　　　the drum,
　　At a minute or two to two, today, at a minute
　　　　or two to two.

A Proper Pot of Coffee

> All I want is a proper cup of coffee,
> Brewed in a proper copper coffee pot.
> I (*pause*) may (*pause*) be off my dot,
> But I want a cup of coffee from a proper copper
>   coffee pot,
> Tin coffee pots and iron coffee pots
> They're no good to me (*clap clap*)
> If I can't have a cup of coffee from a proper
>   copper coffee pot,
> I'll have a cup of tea.

Betty Botter

> Betty Botter bought some butter,
> 'But,' she said, 'this butter's bitter!
> If I put it in my batter,
> It will make my batter bitter,
> But a bit of better butter
> That would make my batter better.'
> So she bought a bit of butter
> Better than her bitter butter,
> And she put it in her batter
> And the batter was not bitter.
> So 'twas better Betty Botter
> Bought a bit of better butter.

In order to help the group remember a tongue twister, split them into teams and allocate a line per group. Ask them to come up with a movement or gesture sequence that illuminates the line; e.g. 'Betty Botter bought some butter' becomes 'Betty (hands on left hip) Botter (hand on right hip) bought (mime giving a coin) some butter (hold out hands as if taking the butter).' The whole class can either learn the sequence, or you can perform the tongue twister as a dance, with each group performing their line in order. Then try taking out the words and see if the group can maintain the rhythm of the tongue twister in their silent mime dance.

The Aim of the Game

To warm up the voice and emphasise articulation in an active and exciting way.

Players	Age	Time	Skills
Any number	8+	10	Memory, Rhythm

Radio Shuffle

A quick-fire voice game that involves players improvising extracts from radio broadcasts when the 'dial' moves their way.

How to Play

Ask the group to stand in a circle. You stand in the middle of the ring with your arms pointing outwards, hands together, ready to point at any of the players.

The idea is simple. You are the radio dial, and whenever you point at someone, their channel is playing. They must improvise a snippet from a radio broadcast, and keep going until the dial moves on to someone else. You might keep the dial on them for as little as a second, or for an extended period if you like the sound of their show.

Get the players to brainstorm types of radio show in advance. There may be a news broadcast (they can make this as comic as they like), *Gardener's Question Time*, public debate, a quiz show, drama, classical or pop music stations, a political broadcast, adverts, the Shipping Forecast, a public announcement, hobby shows, an intellectual discussion, a celebrity interview, a cookery documentary... the more inventive their ideas, the better.

Remind them that you usually join a broadcast part way through when you tune in, so they may like to start halfway through a sentence or in the middle of an announcement. Ask them to think of their first idea before you start, to avoid pauses during the game. Once the dial has left them, they should think of a different idea for the next time the dial points at them, in order to become several channels during the course of the game. This also avoids stop-starts while you wait for people to think of an idea.

The Aim of the Game

The aim is to achieve a fast-paced, fluent response with no gaps for 'thinking time'. The game encourages vocal creativity and originality without the pressure of using the body, so it is an excellent starting point for exploring the importance of voice in performance.

It also encourages spontaneity and focus, as players never know when the dial is coming, or for how long it will be tuned in to their stations.

Variations and Extensions

You can also play a 'television' version of this game. Players stand in a line and have to jump into the space and begin improvising a TV show whenever you ring a bell. However, the joy of the radio version is that it allows you to concentrate on the voice alone, focusing on expression, accent, modulation and projection, without the pressures of incorporating body language and gesture. The television version is better for workshops on improvisation and character, rather than voice specifically.

Players	Age	Time	Skills
6+	10+	10	*Focus, Improvisation, Spontaneity*

Soundscapes

A creative game in which players create sound pictures to illustrate a scene.

How to Play

A 'soundscape' is a vocal version of a landscape, a 'sound picture' that attempts to capture the atmosphere of a place, theme or a concept through noises. There are many ways to use soundscapes in drama; they can be effective right from primary-school drama to degree-level performance work and devising.

Divide the group into teams of at least six players. Choose a theme or a place as the stimulus. You may wish to give each group a different stimulus, or to set everyone the same challenge in order to explore the variations on a theme.

For young players, pick simple places with known animals or familiar noises. For instance, choose a farmyard, beach, jungle, woodland or outer space. You might like to allocate specific sound effects to individuals before you begin, if working with very young players.

Fantasy scenes work well with slightly older groups, a haunted house or a pirate ship, for instance. Alternatively, pick a dramatic climate scene, like a storm, or simply give them an emotion to explore, which you could link into character work later on in the session.

With older groups, it is interesting to offer them an abstract word or concept; e.g. blue, foe, fan, shoot. The responses to such open-ended stimuli are often fascinating and reveal the nuances of a single word's multiple connotations.

When you have allocated your theme, ask each group to choose a conductor. It is advisable to take this role yourself with younger players. The conductor will lead the group, taking responsibility for the overall shape of the piece. They bring individuals in, one by one, indicate volume and dynamics using hand gestures, and show the group when to finish.

Give the groups a chance to rehearse their

soundscapes and then ask the teams to listen to each other with their eyes closed. You might then ask the listeners to identify all the sounds they heard, and to say what they enjoyed about the soundscape.

The Aim of the Game

This is an inventive and dynamic way to explore sound effects and vocal qualities with a group. It encourages the group to create a composition as a group, and often results in impressive work. It can also be a creative starting point for building improvisation scenes, and a useful tool for devising.

Variations and Extensions

Whilst younger groups should be encouraged to use sound effects rather than dialogue and words, you might like to include speech if working with older players. Creating a lunchtime café soundscape, for instance, can become a fascinating piece of drama, fading in and out of conversations. This can be used as an initial exercise for exploring crosscutting as a convention in devised scenes, where the focus moves between several scenes.

Players	Age	Time	Skills
6+	6+	15	*Imagination, Teamwork*

Human Orchestra

A creative rhythm game for older players, in which they attempt to create a dynamic piece of music using vocal sounds.

How to Play

To play the simple version, allocate each player a rhythm within a four-beat frame. For example:

JO:	1	2	*Pause*	4.
BECCA:	1	*Pause*	3 and	4.
EWAN:	*Pause*	*Pause*	*Pause*	4.
RUSSELL:	1 and a 2 and a 3		4.	

Ask the players to choose how they are going to create their sound, either singing, clapping, stamping, etc. The conductor (you or a competent player) then leads them through their piece, bringing players in and out, one by one, to create different effects in the music. The conductor can also change the volume by indicating upwards or downwards with a simple hand gesture. Alternatively, you can ask the players to choose their own rhythms.

A further adaptation of this game is to ask players to choose instruments from an orchestra, and to create sounds mimicking their chosen instruments to create a more vibrant sound.

The Aim of the Game

This exercise encourages competence with rhythm and timing, as well as giving the group an opportunity to create an inventive piece as a team. This may be a good exercise to use in preparation for work on verse or Shakespeare, as it encourages an exploration of different rhythmic effects and patterns.

Players	Age	Time	Skills
6+	**8+**	**15**	*Imagination, Rhythm, Focus*

Good Evening, Your Majesty

An imaginative game in which players have to think of an interesting voice to disguise their identities.

How to Play

Before you begin this game, ensure that everyone knows each other's names. You could premise this game with one of the name games from Part Two: Familiarity, in order to help the players to identify each other.

Choose one person to be 'up', let's call him Matt. Matt must stand at one end of the room with his back to the rest of the group, who are assembled in a line at the other end. Then indicate, without words, someone from the line-up to step forward, let's call her Emma. In her funniest voice, Emma says 'Good evening, Your Majesty.' Matt then has to guess who the mystery voice was. Once he has guessed, he turns round to see who the voice belonged to. If he gets it right, Emma is 'up' and becomes the guesser. If not, Matt must turn his back again and someone else is chosen as the mystery voice.

The Aim of the Game

This game provides an opportunity for players to experiment with characterisation of their voices in a light-hearted, explorative way.

Players	Age	Time	Skills
Any number	**6+**	**5**	*Imagination, Character*

Sing-along Word Association

A hilarious game that involves players jumping in with song ideas, a great game for aspiring musical theatre or karaoke stars!

How to Play

Ask the group to stand in a circle. Explain that this game is about quick thinking and word association, rather than quality of singing, so those who think they 'can't sing' need not worry!

One player begins by running into the middle of the circle and singing a song of their choice. The song can be anything, from a nursery rhyme to a pop song. The others must listen carefully. As soon as one of the other players hears a word that appears in the lyrics of a different song, then they run in and replace the singer, beginning their new song on the word they heard.

A typical game might go something like this:

DUNCAN: And I will always love *you* –

EFFIE: *You* make me feel mighty real,
You make me *feel* –

NAOMI: *Feel*ing good, na, na, na, na, na, na,
Birds in the sky, you *know* –

ROHAN: *Know*ing me, knowing you, a-ha
There is nothing we can't *do* –

JESS: *Do* wa diddy, diddy-dum, diddy-do,
There she was,
Just a-walking down the street...

And so on and so forth.

The Aim of the Game

This is a great energy-building vocal game, which helps to warm up the voice and to build confidence. Because there are often players ready to jump in with an idea, each player's turn is usually so short that initial nerves about singing in front of the group are soon disbanded.

Players	Age	Time	Skills
6+	10+	10	*Imagination, Spontaneity, Confidence*

PART TWO

FAMILIARITY

FAMILIARITY

Anyone Who...

An energetic familiarisation game to help a group get to know each other.

How to Play

In this game, players get to know random information about each other in a fun and energetic way. The game format is similar to *Fruit Salad* (Game 31), but the objectives are different, as follows.

Choose one player to be 'up', and ask everyone else to sit on a chair in a circle, with the chosen player in the centre. The player in the middle calls out 'Anyone who...' followed by a fact of their choice; e.g. 'Anyone who is a girl!' Everyone who the fact applies to then jumps up and swaps places with each other as quickly as possible. Meanwhile, the player who called out the category also runs for one of the available seats. Whoever is left without a seat is then in the centre, and calls the next 'Anyone who...'

When playing with younger players, you might like suggest categories like clothing and appearance; e.g. 'Anyone who has blue eyes' or 'Anyone who is wearing red.'

With older players the game can be more revealing, with questions like 'Anyone who has visited Africa' or 'Anyone who has read a Harry Potter book.'

The Aim of the Game

Whilst this game is an energetic warm-up game, perhaps its greatest asset is that it allows the group to get to know a bit more about each other. It is an excellent starter activity with a new group.

Players	Age	Time	Skills
6+	6+	10	*Energy, Focus, Listening*

Red Ball, Yellow Ball

A challenging name game, which demands energy, focus and tongue-twisting skills.

How to Play

Ask the players to stand in a circle. One player, let's call her Ella, begins by miming throwing an imaginary ball to someone across the circle, let's say Ben. As she does so, she says 'Red ball, Ben.' Ben pretends to catch the imaginary ball, saying 'Red Ball, thank you' as he does so, and then 'Red Ball, Joe' as he passes the imaginary ball on to Joe. The game continues, as the players mime passing and catching the ball in rhythm, as the dialogue gets faster and faster:

ELLA: *(Throwing.)* Red ball, Ben.

BEN: *(Catching.)* Red ball, thank you.
 (Throwing.) Red ball, Joe.

JOE: *(Catching.)* Red ball, thank you.
 (Throwing.) Red ball, Ollie...

When the players have got the hang of passing the red ball quickly and efficiently, you can introduce a new imaginary ball, a yellow ball, which works on exactly the same principles. Players then have to concentrate on which ball is where! If both balls get passed to the same player simultaneously, he or she must accept them both before passing them on to different players:

JOE: *(Catching in left hand.)* Red ball, thank you.
 (Catching in right hand.) Yellow ball,
 thank you.
 (Throwing.) Red ball, Romilly.
 (Throwing.) Yellow ball, Harry.

You can introduce as many different coloured balls as your group can cope with! This is a very good pre-performance game to get actors focused.

The Aim of the Game

The aim is for the group to maintain a consistent and energised rhythm, and to help the group become familiar with each other's names.

Players	Age	Time	Skills
Any number	**8+**	**5**	*Energy, Focus, Listening*

Name Tag

A quick and competitive name game that helps a group get to know each other in an active and exciting way.

How to Play

This game is similar to the playground game *Tag*. Ask the players to find a space in the room. Choose one person to be 'up', let's call her Laura. All the other players must stand frozen in their places, only Laura is allowed to move.

Laura's aim is to tag another player before they have time to call out someone else's name. For instance, Laura walks towards Ben. If Ben is quick thinking and shouts out 'Alice' before Laura gets to him, then Alice is 'up' and Laura simply stops where she is and joins in as another player. However, if Ben is slow and Laura reaches him before he has time to shout out a name, then he is out. Thus the number of players gets smaller and smaller, and the game gets quicker and more difficult.

The Aim of the Game

This game demands quick thinking and excellent awareness skills. Everyone must stay focused on who is 'in' and who is out, in order to shout an appropriate name as quickly as possible. It certainly helps new groups get to know each other's names very quickly.

Variations and Extensions

To make the game even more challenging, try this additional factor. When a player is caught out, they must stand against the wall at one end of the room, forming a line with the other players who are out. Every time someone joins this line, the whole line moves forward one pace. The line soon becomes a moving boundary, a fourth wall, which makes the playing space smaller and the game both faster and more difficult for the remaining players!

Players	Age	Time	Skills
10+	**10+**	**10**	*Energy, Focus, Name Recognition*

The Amazing 'A's Game

A quick warm-up game for younger players, involving introducing themselves to the group, name familiarisation and basic mime skills.

How to Play

Ask the players to sit in a circle. They must all think of an activity that begins with the same letter as their first name. When everyone has thought of an activity, the game can start. One at a time, the players must stand up (you can stand with them if they are very young) and introduce themselves.

To use an example, let's say Stan goes first. He says 'My name is Stan and I like…' at which point he mimes doing underwater movements, swimming around the circle. The others must then guess what Stan's activity is. Sally puts her hand up and guesses swimming, but Stan shakes his head. Jean guesses snorkelling, but Stan shakes his head again. Nikki then guesses scuba-diving, which was right, so now it is Nikki's turn.

Alternatively, you can ask everyone in the circle to call out the answer together. In this case, go round the circle to do the introductions, rather than choosing who is next by who guesses correctly. You may also need to help younger players with unusual names to think of appropriate activities!

The Aim of the Game

The game encourages confidence in younger players, and gives them the opportunity to act something simple out in front of the other players.

Players	Age	Time	Skills
Any number	**6+**	**10**	*Confidence, Mime, Name Recognition*

Elbow to Elbow

A warm-up game encouraging physical contact between players; a good icebreaker for new casts and classes.

How to Play

This is a game in two parts: the first involves experimenting with ways of moving, and the second, working with a partner to find interesting physical positions.

Ask the players to find a space. Set them off by asking them to move around the room in a specific way. You could choose any theme; e.g. pick particular characters (royalty, scheming criminals, air hostesses), emotions (joy, sadness, jealousy) or ask them to move through a specified terrain (across the baking hot desert, through deep jelly). Try and choose a theme that relates to the rest of your workshop or rehearsal. For instance, if you are running a workshop on *A Midsummer Night's Dream*, you could ask them to move as the characters (fairies, mechanicals, lovers), or as if in an appropriate location (in Theseus' court, in an enchanted wood, at a royal wedding).

Once everyone is confidently moving around in that style, shout out two body parts; e.g. 'Elbow to elbow.' Each player must run to the person nearest them and make a position in which those two parts are touching. Once everyone has done so, set them off again with a new way of walking. The game continues, as you suggest each new style of moving, followed by a new combination of body parts. Some combinations are more challenging than others; for instance, head to toe, or ear to knee. This can lead to some amusing poses. Obviously sensitivity in choosing body parts here is important for reasons of both safety and embarrassment!

The Aim of the Game

The game encourages both familiarity with others in the group and exploration of physical movement and character.

Variations and Extensions

Both parts of this game can be played independently of each other. I enjoy combining the two focuses in order to explore a wider range of skills.

A further variation, which is a great tool for encouraging players to form groups, is to call out numbers instead of body parts. On hearing the number, players must run into groups of that number of players, sitting down as soon as they have the right number. This is an inventive way to get them into teams with people outside their own friendship group.

Players	Age	Time	Skills
8+	6+	10	*Teamwork, Focus, Energy, Character*

I Love You, Honey!

An all-time favourite amongst many actors and drama students, this is a comic game in which the aim is to avoid the urge to laugh.

How to Play

Choose someone to be 'up', let's call her Jill. Jill chooses someone across the circle as her target, e.g. Robin. She must cross the circle in a dramatic and amusing way, and say to him 'I love you, honey!' in the funniest manner possible. Robin must answer 'I love you too, but I just can't smile!' – without smiling! If he smiles or laughs, then he is 'up', and Jill takes his place in the circle. If, however, he controls himself and doesn't smile, Jill has to try again on someone else.

Encourage the players to be as inventive as possible when trying to make their targets laugh. Use funny walks, body language and voices. Often the funniest deliveries are when a specific character is portrayed; e.g. a cuckold, a flasher, a seductive movie star or a Spanish lover.

The Aim of the Game

The aim is to create fun and exciting characters, and to help players learn how to control themselves on stage. By linking this to the idea of 'corpsing', you can stress the importance of staying focused during a performance.

Players	Age	Time	Skills
Any number	10+	5	Focus, Imagination, Improvisation, Self-control

PART THREE

ENERGY

Energy Ball

A favourite warm-up game amongst my non-English-speaking actors in the Marshall Islands, this game needs no words – just actions, sound and lots and lots of energy!

How to Play

Ask the players to stand in a circle. Explain that you are going to pass round a ball of energy, which will fade and die if you don't pass it on with enough enthusiasm.

Now pass the imaginary ball across the circle, using a spontaneous sound effect and movement, the more strange and inventive, the better. The person receiving the ball has to make the same sound effect when catching it, then pass it on with a new sound effect and movement. This game quickly gets the whole group moving and enjoying themselves, as the sound effects and movements become more outlandish.

The Aim of the Game

The aim is to increase and focus everyone's energy, encourage creativity, and get each individual involved. Encourage them to find unusual means of throwing the imaginary ball; e.g. skim it, bounce it, boomerang it, send it off like a rocket... whatever they can come up with.

Players	Age	Time	Skills
Any number	6+	5	Voice, Quick Responses, Movement, Teamwork

Splat!

A favourite game in many youth theatre companies, this is a drama version of Shoot 'Em Up! *that encourages concentration... and fits of the giggles!*

How to Play

Ask the players to stand in a circle. You stand in the middle of the circle as the Sheriff (once the players become familiar with the game, they can easily take this role). Everyone stands with their hands on their imaginary holsters.

All of a sudden, you point your imaginary gun at one of the players, let's call him Jim, and say 'Splat!' Jim then ducks. Immediately, the players on either side of Jim, Joe and Emma, point their imaginary guns at each other and say 'Splat!' as fast as they can. Whoever said it first – in this case, Emma – is the winner. Joe loses a life and therefore kneels up on one knee. After his next loss, he will kneel up on two knees. The third time he will be out, and therefore must sit down on the floor, cross-legged. Players may also lose a life if they forget to duck when the Sheriff fires at them.

The game continues until there are only two players left, at which point, it is time for the shoot-off. Ask the two players to stand back to back in the centre of the circle. Count to 3 and ask them to take one step away from each other, remaining back to back, on each number.

Now ask the other players to suggest a 'magic word'. Once you have chosen one, begin telling a brief story. At some point (before too long), use the magic word in the tale. As soon as they hear the word, the two players must turn and 'splat' each other. Whoever is the quickest wins!

The Aim of the Game

The game encourages speed and concentration, the aim is to be faster than everyone else to win the shoot-off.

Players	Age	Time	Skills
8+	6+	10	*Focus, Awareness, Quick Responses*

Whoosh!

A physical, high-energy game that gets the group to focus using sound effects and simple movements.

How to Play

Ask the players to stand in a circle. Begin by teaching the basic rules, trying each one out, one by one, as follows.

The 'whoosh' is an imaginary ball. To pass the 'whoosh' around the circle in a single direction, make a throwing motion towards the person next to you and say 'Whoosh!' as you do so. Practise passing this round the whole circle until it comes back to you. 'Whooshes' can only move in one continuous direction and cannot move across the circle.

The next movement to learn is 'zap', which reverses the direction of the 'whoosh'. Cross your arms in an X-shape in front of you and say 'Zap!' in order to send the 'whoosh' back the way it came. The person who 'whooshed' it to you has to then 'whoosh' it back the other way.

The third movement is 'bazoom', which passes the 'whoosh' to someone on the other side of the circle. To do this point at them using both hands, as if firing a gun, and say 'Bazoom!' in an appropriately booming voice.

The key rules are as follows: 'Whoosh!' to pass it along, 'Zap!' to send it back and 'Bazoom!' to throw it across the room. Try and avoid getting the 'whoosh' stuck between two people who keep 'zapping' it between each other! You cannot 'zap' a 'bazoom'. You can 'bazoom' a 'bazoom'.

Get the players to play with the 'whoosh' as quickly and energetically as possible, reversing directions, sending it to and fro, around and across the circle. When they have mastered this, you can add a second 'whoosh'!

The Aim of the Game

The game encourages the group to work together, building a rhythm and following instructions exactly.

Variations and Extensions

There are infinite variations of this game, using different hand movements and sound effects. Adapt and experiment as you please to create themed versions: Under the Sea and Jungle themes work particularly well with younger players. Simply substitute each movement and sound with a new one, appropriate to the theme ('wave', 'splash' and 'splosh', for instance). For a detailed and elaborate adaptation of this game, try *Yeehah!* (Game 29).

If you are playing this game with a group that meets regularly, you can also add further rules as the weeks go on. Think of a movement and sound to allow the 'whoosh' to skip a person, or skip two places. You can also add a movement that entails everyone swapping places with each other.

For an added level of difficulty, try asking everyone to slowly move round, thus rotating the circle, whilst continuing to play the game.

Players	Age	Time	Skills
6+	6+	5	*Focus, Dynamism, Quick Responses*

Yeehah!

A Wild West-themed circle game, which heightens energy and gets a group to exercise both body and voice.

How to Play

This game has a similar premise to *Whoosh!* (Game 28), requiring players to memorise the rules of passing the energy. This particular game is enjoyable because of the theme, and because it incorporates a whole array of actions.

Players stand in a circle. Begin by passing a 'yeehah' around the circle to the left. To 'yeehah', simply swing your arm across your body, as if swinging an imaginary beer keg, yelling 'Yeehah!' Practise passing this movement energetically from player to player all the way around the circle. You must always swing your arm across your body in the direction the 'yeehah' is traveling in.

Now introduce the second rule. To change the direction of the 'yeehah', you say 'Hoedown!', whilst making a pulling-down motion with the arm on the opposite side to the 'yeehah'; e.g. if the 'yeehah' approaches from your right, your 'hoedown' motion must happen with your left arm. This sends the 'yeehah' back the other way.

To pass the 'yeehah' across the circle, aim your arm like a gun, and make a firing noise, making it clear who you are aiming at, so they can then pass the 'yeehah' round.

Whilst these three rules make the game sufficiently complicated for young players, you can add several exciting new rules for more advanced players.

Firstly, you can add the ability to skip a player. Say 'Hay Barn!' arching your arms above your head like the roof of a barn, and the 'yeehah' skips your neighbour and passes to the next person round.

Secondly, you can skip a player and change direction by saying 'Cowgirl!' in a girly voice, whilst doing a curtsey. This skips it back one in the opposite direction.

Thirdly, you can shout 'Cowboy!' At this point,

everyone pretends to jump onto a horse and rides across the circle, changing positions and reforming the circle in a different order. Whoever shouted this command then begins the next 'yeehah' to avoid losing the momentum.

The Aim of the Game

The game encourages a high level of focus and teamwork, and requires memory skills from its players, particularly when harder rules are introduced.

Variations and Extensions

I have sometimes played this game for several weeks in a row, adding a new rule each session, and encouraging the group to come up with their own new rules. This is an exciting way of making the game more challenging and helping the players invest creatively in their activities.

Players	Age	Time	Skills
8+	8+	5	*Focus, Memory, Teamwork, Dynamism*

ENERGY

Duck, Duck, Goose!

*A favourite game amongst schoolchildren in Britain –
a game of chase, with a little added creativity.*

How to Play

Ask the players to sit in a circle. Ensure the circle is
far enough away from the walls that players can
safely run around the outside without injuring
themselves.

Choose one player to be 'up', let's call him
Duncan. Duncan chooses two contrasting nouns,
e.g. 'duck' and 'goose'. He then walks slowly
around the edge of the circle, patting each player
on the head and saying 'Duck' as he does. At some
point he chooses one player to be 'Goose', let's
call her Verena.

When Duncan touches her head and says 'Goose',
Verena must jump up and chase him around the
outside of the circle. His aim is to get back to her
empty spot and sit down before she touches him. If
he is successful, then he takes her place in the
circle. However, if she catches him, he has to sit in
'the duck pond' (the middle of the circle) for three
goes. Verena is 'up' next. She chooses her own two
words (perhaps 'lion' and 'tiger'), and the game
continues.

The Aim of the Game

The game encourages speed of movement and
imagination, as the young players choose their own
contrasting words.

Variations and Extensions

Try a more dramatic version of the standard game
by specifying animals as the category and asking the
players to run as their chosen animals when they
are chased or chasing round the circle.

You can also specify a theme that matches the focus
of your workshop. If you are devising a play set in a
haunted house, for instance, you could choose pairs
like 'ghost' and 'ghoul', 'skeleton' and 'bone', 'night'
and 'owl'.

My favourite version of this game, known as *Drip, Drip, Drop!*, is strictly reserved to open-air summertime sessions, as it involves getting wet! The leader has a bucket and each round fills a cup with water. The player who is 'up' has to drip a little drip of water onto each player's head, saying 'Drip' as they do, before choosing someone to 'drop' on, at which point they empty the cup over the unsuspecting victim's head! The soaked player then chases after them and the game continues as before. This needs to be closely regulated and is more suited to the end of a long summer day's session when the players are overheated and need a quick release, rather than part of a focused drama class!

Players	Age	Time	Skills
8+	6+	5	Movement, Imagination, Pacing

ENERGY

Fruit Salad

An energetic focus game, requiring players to move when their 'fruit' group is called.

How to Play

Divide the players into groups of approximately four, and ask each group to choose a fruit. Next, ask them to announce their fruit to the rest of the class. Then ask them to rejoin as a whole group, mix themselves up, and sit in a circle on chairs.

Now, choose one player to be 'up', let's call him Vinny. Ask Vinny to stand in the middle of the circle, then remove his chair, so that there is one less chair than the number of players. Vinny then calls out the name of one of the fruits chosen. All the players from that fruit group must jump up and swap places with each other as quickly as possible. Meanwhile, Vinny also runs for one of the available seats. Whoever is left without a seat is then 'up', and calls the next fruit type.

If the person in the centre calls 'Fruit Salad!', everyone has to get up and find a new seat, regardless of their individual fruit type.

The Aim of the Game

The game encourages speedy reactions and good listening skills, the aim is to stay seated and to avoid being 'up'.

Variations and Extensions

This game can easily be adapted to suit any theme, and works well in school drama classes when exploring a specific subject; for instance, you could use or and famous historical figures as categories.

Players	Age	Time	Skills
6+	**6+**	**5**	*Focus, Listening, Quick Responses*

Shark Attack!

A fast-paced warm-up game for younger players, involving animal characterisation and quick thinking.

How to Play

Place chairs around the room, one less than the number of players. When you call out 'Swim!', the players move around the room as fish, with smooth, gliding movements and appropriate facial expressions. At any interval you may shout out 'Shark!' On hearing this, the players must dart to 'safety' (sit on a chair). The player with no seat is out, and then must choose the next sea creature for the group to mime – jellyfish, whales, dolphins, crabs and sea snakes are good options. Another chair is removed so another player will be out each round until there is a winner.

To keep the group on their toes you can shout out red herrings (no pun intended), non-dangerous or fictional animals, like a 'Banana fish' or 'Can of tuna'. If they sit down on one of these, they are also out.

To add an extra level of excitement, you may choose to shout out other dangerous animals like 'Swordfish' or 'Electric eel'. This encourages the players to think carefully, and quickly, about whether the fish are dangerous or not.

The Aim of the Game

Whilst this game encourages speedy reactions, the dramatic focus is on characterisation. Encourage the players to use both face and body and voices to portray the specific creatures.

Variations and Extensions

You can easily vary this game to explore other environments. In *Jungle Boogie*, for instance, the monkeys, sloths and anteaters must escape from the jaguar, and in *Sahara, Sahara*, the lion threatens to eat the gazelles, emus and wildebeest. Other potential themes include Space and Hogwarts.

Players	Age	Time	Skills
6+	6+	10	*Imagination, Listening, Focus, Mime*

Captain Cod

A quick and easy energy game, a pirate version of
Simon Says.

How to Play

This is a fun game for younger players, who, in my
experience, often become addicted to it! This game
requires more of the players than the traditional
Simon Says because they have to remember a
specific vocabulary of movements, all of which
relate to the theme. For this reason, you might like
to use this as a warm-up for a session that
incorporates dance or requires the group to
remember movement sequences.

The game is set on a pirate ship, where Captain
Cod (you) gives instructions. If you say 'Captain
Cod says…', the group must do the action. If you
do not say 'Captain Cod says…' and just tell them
the instruction, then they must *not* do it! You can
choose whether those who make a mistake are out
or whether to keep everyone in to avoid bored
players. Explain each of the actions to the group
before you start.

The actions are as follows:

Climb the rigging – *Mime climbing up ropes.*

Scrub the deck – *Mime scrubbing the floor.*

Mrs Cod's coming! – *Mime acting as Mrs Cod,
hands on hips, wolf-whistling.*

Walk the plank – *Mime walking along the plank.*

Fire the cannon – *Mime getting on your knees
and making an explosive sound.*

Captain's parrot – *Mime flapping your wings,
saying 'Pretty Polly' in a parrot-like voice.*

Man overboard! – *Mime diving into the water,
making a 'splosh' sound.*

Two men overboard! – *Mime diving into the
water and swim to a partner.*

Three men overboard! – *Mime diving into the
water and swim into a three, etc.*

X marks the spot – *Freeze!*

The Aim of the Game

The aim is to encourage the players to follow the instructions carefully and listen to the Captain. The activities encourage the group to be energetic and focused in their actions.

Variations and Extensions

With younger groups, I often play a 'Harry Potter' version of this game, which is great fun and popular with both boys and girls. The same rules apply: if 'Potter says' do it, you do it! Actions can include:

Catch the golden snitch – *Mime catching a ball.*

Hermione's study – *Mime writing a spell.*

The Hogwart's Express – *Mime being a train, saying 'Choo, choo!'*

Wizard duel – *Mime taking part in a battle with imaginary partner.*

Slytherin – *Mime being a creepy member of this scheming house, silently rubbing your hands together as if plotting Harry's downfall.*

Gryffindor – *Mime walking proudly with your hands on your hips.*

Dobby the house elf – *Mime moving around the room in an elf-like way, picking up your feet and twiddling your fingers.*

You can add as many other actions as you wish and choose an appropriate theme according to the interests of the players.

Players	Age	Time	Skills
6+	6+	10	Listening, Movement, Memory

Penguin Race

A very silly and lovable game that involves the whole group in a thigh-slapping, quick-fire, action-based race.

How to Play

In this energetic and amusing game, the group have to follow each of your instructions to complete the penguin race, during which you commentate, telling them which obstacles are coming up, and encourage them to go as fast as possible. Begin by getting the whole group to stand facing you. Tell them that you are all about to take part in the Grand Penguin Race, and your entire team (the group) is in the final! You have to complete the race course together.

Now lead them through the mimed sequence of preparations for the race. Firstly, put on your crash helmets, your snow goggles, your speed gloves, extra-thick scarf, body protector, race boots and race number. Then teach the team each of the actions (below) that they will need to perform when they hear that instruction. To 'run', the players stand and (gently!) slap their thighs, to make the sound of a penguin running along, like making a drumroll sound on your lap. The whole game takes place on the spot, so they must avoid moving out of their places. They need to continue this action throughout the game, in between each obstacle, until you say the race is over.

Whilst they are 'running', you give the team various instructions as you encounter each imaginary obstacle. My standard obstacles are as follows, but each group always has a plethora of extra obstacles they like to suggest as they become familiar with the game.

> Turns to the left or right – *Make a swooping movement to the side in question.*
>
> Snow jump – *Jump up in the air saying 'Woo!'*
>
> Low bridge – *Duck down, with your hands on your head to protect yourself.*
>
> Slalom – *Make a weaving motion with your knees to the left and right.*

Water jump – *Jump up in the air – 'Woo!' – then make a 'splosh' noise when you land.*

Wave to the Queen – *Say 'Hello, Ma'am!', waving in a deferent manner to the right.*

Wave to the crowd – *Say 'Yeah!' and make a thumbs-up gesture to the left.*

Snowboard – *Act as if you are snowboarding and sing the* Batman *theme tune, changing the words to 'Na na na na, na na na na, na na na na, na na na na – Penguin!'*

Steep climb – *Lean back, looking up, saying 'Woooaaahhh!'*

Over the top – *Leaning forward, circling your arms as if skiing too fast, saying 'Aargh!'*

Once the group know each of these actions, the game is quite simple. You say '1, 2, 3 – Go!' On the word 'Go!' they begin slapping their thighs. Talk them through the race, adding obstacles as you go:

And they're off… the penguins are racing down the hill, they're coming up to a water jump – 'Woo! – splosh!' – and there's a slalom, oh look – wave to the Queen… etc.

When you get to the finish line, everyone should cheer!

The Aim of the Game

The game is most effective in building a team as it is such an energetic group activity. You can all celebrate together when you 'win' the race!

Players	Age	Time	Skills
Any number	6+	15	Teamwork, Listening, Memory, Movement

King of the Jungle

The favourite warm-up game amongst our actors in Red Handed Theatre Company, this game is a hilarious test of memory, coordination and speed, which involves memorising an amazing array of animal movements and noises in sequence!

How to Play

Ask the group to stand in a semicircle. Each of the players is designated a position in the animal kingdom, from the lion as King of the Jungle at one end of the semicircle, to the humble amoeba at the opposite end. Each animal has a sound and an action. Before you begin, make sure the entire group knows the order, sounds and actions of all the animals from the top of the hierarchy to the bottom.

A potential 'Animal Kingdom' for ten players is as follows, although you can change or add to this list as you wish:

1. Lion
   Sound: 'Roooaarrr!'
   Movement: Hands as claws

2. Elephant
   Sound: Trumpeting sound
   Movement: Use arm as a trunk

3. Orangutan
   Sound: 'Oooaaaaahhhh!'
   Movement: Beating chest

4. Crocodile
   Sound: 'Snap, snap!'
   Movement: Use arms extended out as snapping jaws

5. Horse
   Sound: 'Neigh!'
   Movement: Shaking head as if tossing mane

6. Monkey
   Sound: 'Oo-ooh, aa-aaah!'
   Movement: Hands in armpits

7. Fish
   Sound: 'Splosh!'
   Movement: Make a motion as if diving into the water

8. Mouse
   Sound: 'Eeee-eee!'
   Movement: Use hands as whiskers in front of face

9. Worm
   Sound: 'Wiggle, wiggle!'
   Movement: Use one finger as a wiggling worm

10. Amoeba
   Sound: 'Blob, blob, blob!'
   Movement: Turn round, wiggling like a jellyfish

To play the game, the King of the Jungle (the lion) begins by doing his sound and action, followed immediately by someone else's; for instance, the crocodile's: 'Roooaar – Snap, snap!' The crocodile must then follow immediately by repeating his own sound and action, followed by someone else's: 'Snap, snap – Neigh!' , which is the horse's cue: 'Neigh – Wiggle, wiggle!', and so on.

If anyone makes a mistake, either by being too slow or by getting the combination of sound and actions wrong, they are sent to the bottom of the food chain and become the amoeba. Anyone who was between them and the bottom therefore moves up one role. The game is challenging because every mistake entails players shifting positions to take on a new animal. Aim to make the game as fast-paced as possible, and encourage the players to make their sounds and actions energetic.

The Aim of the Game

The aim is to get a sequence running as quickly and energetically as possible without making a mistake. This not only requires concentration from each of the players, but the ability to focus and work together as a team. This is an outstanding game for promoting energy and group coordination, and is definitely one of my favourites.

Players	Age	Time	Skills
10-20	8+	10	*Focus, Memory, Pacing, Coordination*

Character Corners

A simple dancing game which is great for improving movement skills.

How to Play

Choose a theme appropriate to the workshop you are leading; for example, Space. Label each of the four corners of the room with a different themed name; e.g. 'Moon', 'Sun', 'Spaceship' and 'Black Hole'. Bring appropriate music, in this case, perhaps *The Planets* by Gustav Holst, '90s hit 'Spaceman' by Babylon Zoo, or some modern electronic music that sounds futuristic.

Explain to the group that you are going to ask them to move around as specific objects or characters within the theme; e.g. aliens or spacemen. Ask them to think about the speed, dynamics and style of the movement, to help them create detailed characterisations. They must move in character the whole time. Play the CD and guide the group through the game, encouraging them to use the music to help enhance their characterisations. At a certain point, stop the music and look away. They must then silently run to one of the four corners. Ensuring you do not look round, call out one of the four corners at random. Whoever is at that corner is out, and can help to choose the next character type. Continue the game until you have a winner.

The Aim of the Game

The aim is to create characters in a fun, themed context, and to add an element of risk with the threat of getting 'out'. Ensure that you use the players who are out to observe the others moving carefully, and to suggest future characterisations, so that they stay involved in the activity.

+ Recorded music			
Players	**Age**	**Time**	**Skills**
10+	6+	10	*Movement, Rhythm, Character*

PART FOUR

FOCUS

Mexican Clap

A game of speed and teamwork… pass the clap before the clock! I often use this as an initial exercise with a new group, in order to get them going.

How to Play

Ask the players to stand in a circle, with their hands out in front of them as if they are about to clap them together. Explain that this is a race against the clock, and that you are going to time the speed at which they can pass the clap around the circle, like a Mexican wave. In order to 'pass the clap', they clap their hands towards the person next to them. However, they must wait for their neighbour before they to pass it on… otherwise the circle is broken!

Then begin the game, counting '1, 2, 3 – Go!' Time them each round and, as they get quicker, give them a lap time to aim for. In order to achieve this goal they will have to work as a team and really focus on the task in hand.

The Aim of the Game

This is simply a game of speed and focus, but it creates a great feeling of success and teamwork each time the group manage to knock several seconds off their lap time! When you set them a goal to beat, inevitably they will achieve it (providing you give them a reasonable target!), which is a great boost for the group as a team.

+ Stopwatch			
Players	**Age**	**Time**	**Skills**
10+	6+	5	*Pacing, Teamwork, Energy, Quick Responses*

Eyes Up!

A simple focus game for the beginning of a session.

How to Play

Ask the players to stand in a circle, looking down at the ground. You are going to count to 3 and then say 'Up', at which point they must all raise their heads and look directly at one other player in the circle. Before you begin the count, ask them to decide for themselves who they are going to stare at. The one rule is that they cannot shift their gaze once they have looked up, they must stare at the person they chose in advance. If that person is staring back at them, then both players lose a life.

You can give each player three lives before they are out. On losing the first life, a player kneels down on one knee. On losing a second, they kneel on both knees. On three, they are out and sit cross-legged. The game gets harder as the number of players reduces.

The Aim of the Game

The aim is very simply to quieten and focus a group, and to encourage the players to become comfortable with using eye contact, a useful tool for actors.

Players	Age	Time	Skills
6+	6+	5	*Rhythm, Familiarity, Quick Responses*

FOCUS

Cyclops

A simple focus game for the beginning of a session.

How to Play

This is a popular party game, but it is also effective in classrooms and workshops because it encourages a high level of concentration and an ability to move carefully and quietly.

Place a set of keys underneath a chair in the middle of the circle. Then choose one player to be blindfolded and sit on the chair. This player is the Cyclops, and his job is to listen out for intruders in his cave (the area inside the circle). He must point towards anywhere where he hears a noise. Once Cyclops is blindfolded, choose someone in the circle to be Ulysses. Make sure you select your Ulysses by pointing, so that the Cyclops does not know where in the circle Ulysses will be coming from.

Ulysses' aim is to retrieve the keys from under the chair without being caught (pointed at) by the Cyclops. This requires a very quiet and careful approach. If the Cyclops points at Ulysses, that player must go back to their place in the circle and you choose a new Ulysses. If Ulysses successfully retrieves the keys, then he becomes the Cyclops.

The Aim of the Game

The aim is to achieve a high level of self-control and concentration from each player. This is a silent game, so it is an effective way of focusing and calming a group if you have been doing something very energetic beforehand.

Players	Age	Time	Skills
Any number	**6+**	**10**	*Self-control, Coordination*

Zip, Zap, Zoom!

An extremely simple but effective focus game, great for a quick warm-up at the beginning of a session or before going on stage.

How to Play

The players begin by standing in a circle. Choose someone to start, let's say George. George points with both hands clasped together at someone across the circle (Ross), saying 'Zip!' as he points. Ross then points in the same manner at someone else (Tim) and says 'Zap!' Tim then points at someone else (Cathy) and says 'Zoom!' Cathy points at another player, and says 'Zip!', and the game continues, 'Zip! – Zap! – Zoom! – Zip! – Zap! – Zoom!' As the players gain confidence, the game gets faster.

The Aim of the Game

The aim is for the group to achieve a rapid and regular pace in the repetition of the phrase. For such a simple activity, it is surprising just how effectively this game builds group solidarity and enhances focus levels.

Variations and Extensions

In order to make the game more challenging, you might like to add an action to each of the words. 'Zip!' may be given a whooshing motion, 'Zap!' a throwing gesture, and 'Zoom!' a kick, for example. The chosen actions must be movements that can be directed towards a specific person, to avoid any confusion about which player goes next.

Players	Age	Time	Skills
6+	6+	5	*Energy, Memory, Dynamism*

The Land of Back-to-Front

An effective warm-up game for any age group, in which players must to do the opposite of the instructions given.

How to Play

Ask all the players to find a space. Begin by asking everyone to walk around the room quickly and with purpose, perhaps they are in a hurry to get somewhere, or have something exciting to do. Now introduce the first rules – whenever you say 'Stop', they must freeze immediately. When you say 'Go', they can move again, and continue their fast walk around the room. Practise this a few times.

Then pause the game, and welcome them to the Land of Back-to-Front, where everything means the opposite of what we expect. 'Stop' now means 'Go', and 'Go' means 'Stop'. It is incredible how difficult people find it to reverse their natural reactions to these simple words! Practise a few times with the new instructions.

Once the group has mastered this, you can introduce further commands. Explain that 'Stop' and 'Go' will stay reversed, but that you are going to add two new commands, 'Jump up' and 'Touch the floor'. Begin by playing with these words with their correct meanings, and then you can reverse these too. You can play endless variations of this game, adding new instructions of your own invention. It is surprising how comic the results can be!

The Aim of the Game

The aim is to achieve the high level of concentration necessary in this surprisingly difficult game. The game also encourages players to think for themselves and avoid 'following the herd'. Very often, in the early rounds, when one person moves when they shouldn't, other players will follow suit rather than trusting their own decisions.

Players	Age	Time	Skills
Any number	6+	5	Energy, Self-control

Go Bananas!

A hilarious game for all ages, in which players have to answer 'Bananas' (or an alternative silly word) to every question, without laughing...

How to Play

Choose one player to be 'up', let's call her Muriel. Everyone then thinks of questions to ask Muriel. She must answer every question with the reply 'Bananas', without laughing. If she laughs, whichever player asked the question that made her laugh is 'up', and she returns to the circle.

This game has been the source of many hours of pleasure in workshops I've led. Simple questions like 'What do you brush your teeth with?' or 'What do you keep under your pillow?' often work best. Make sure you ask for 'hands up' when asking for questions from the group.

Every time a new player is 'up', think of a new funny word. Some that have worked well in my workshops include 'Baked beans', 'Shark-infested custard' and, the youngsters' favourite, 'Smelly socks'. 'My boyfriend' or 'My girlfriend' are also popular in older groups ('What do you brush your teeth with?' 'My boyfriend.'), although always ensure you set guidelines for the types of questions allowed at the beginning of the game, to avoid inappropriately rude questions!

The Aim of the Game

The aim is to gain enough control to avoid laughing. This can be linked to actors 'corpsing' and the importance of focus in performance.

Players	Age	Time	Skills
Any number	6+	10	Imagination, Self-control

Relay Rhythms

A simple partner game that emphasises concentration and coordination.

How to Play

This game requires pairs to work together to perform a simple physical and vocal sequence. As the game progresses, spoken numbers are replaced by actions, increasing the need for coordination skills! Ask each player to face their partner. In stage one, the two players count to 3 repeatedly, taking it in turns to say a number. For example:

TOM: 1 –
VICKY: 2 –
TOM: 3 –
VICKY: 1 –
TOM: 2 –
VICKY: 3 – (*etc.*)

Once they have mastered this, pick a pair to demonstrate and ask the group to watch. Then move on to stage two, replacing the word '1' with a click:

TOM: (*He clicks.*)
VICKY: 2 –
TOM: 3 –
VICKY: (*She clicks.*)
TOM: 2 –
VICKY: 3 – (*etc.*)

Again, ask a pair or two to demonstrate their experiences as the game progresses. For the third round, replace the word '2' with a clap. The sequence therefore runs:

TOM: (*He clicks.*)
VICKY: (*She claps.*)
TOM: 3 –
VICKY: (*She clicks, etc.*)

For the final round, '3' is replaced by a stamp, so the sequence becomes: *click, clap, stamp, click, clap, stamp.* When they have completed all four stages, ask the pairs which they found the hardest. Often they will answer the third, because of the combination of speech and action. By the fourth round they are only using actions, which is easier.

The Aim of the Game

The aim is to improve coordination, encouraging the players to use action and voice simultaneously. It is also a helpful exercise to build rapport when working with new partners.

Players	Age	Time	Skills
Any, in pairs	8+	10	Coordination, Teamwork, Familiarity

Meddling Monkey

A simple memory game that requires players to create and memorise a sequence of words and actions.

How to Play

Ask the players to stand in a circle. Explain that you have all recently returned from an exciting exploration into the deepest, darkest Amazon rainforest. As world-class explorers, you were on a mission to record everything you saw. Now, as a group, you are going to remember everything you found in the rainforest.

You then begin the game by saying 'I went into the Amazon and I saw…' followed by an adjective, an animal and an appropriate movement; e.g. flapping your arms as wings, say '…a red macaw.' The next person has to repeat what you said, adding their own animal and action; e.g. 'I went into the jungle and I saw a red macaw (*flapping their arms*) and a slow sloth (*pretending to sleep*).' To make the game a little more challenging, you may wish to insist that the adjective and animal must begin with the same letter; e.g. 'a meddling monkey', 'a jumping jaguar', 'an army ant'. When you have gone round the whole circle once, ask the whole group to perform the entire sequence together. Look how much you have remembered!

The Aim of the Game

The aim is to memorise the entire sequence. You may wish to make a link to the importance of memory for actors, who have many lines to learn.

Variations and Extensions

This game can easily be adapted to fit a theme of your choice. Perhaps you were deep-sea diving, exploring outer space or crossing the mountains.

For younger players, you can structure the game around the alphabet. Choose an easy subject; for instance, 'I went to the shops and I bought…' The first player must think of something beginning with A, the second B, the third C, etc.

For older players, you can ask them to mime their animal for the others to guess. This is an effective way of teaching basic mime skills and often becomes a hilarious activity. Encourage them to perform their mime with as much detail as possible, incorporating sound if they wish. In this version, it is important that they choose familiar animals, otherwise you may end up with a long, tedious round where everyone is stumped trying to guess a pygmy marmoset or other obscure creature, which can prolong the game indefinitely!

Players	Age	Time	Skills
8-20	6+	10	Memory, Imagination, Mime

The Imaginatively Titled Yes-No Game

A game of concentration, control and invention that encourages players to find innovative answers to simple questions.

How to Play

Choose one player to be 'up', let's call her Shahla. Rather like *Go Bananas!* (Game 42), Shahla will be asked questions by everyone else in the group. However, in this game, Shahla must answer every question in the most inventive way, without saying 'Yes' or 'No'. The quicker the other players fire questions at her, the more likely it is that she will be caught out. As soon as she answers 'Yes' or 'No', Shahla is out, and whoever caught her out is 'up'.

At the beginning of the game, give some examples of appropriate questions. Explain that, in order to catch Shahla out, you need to ask her questions which have 'Yes' or 'No' answers; a question like 'How many siblings do you have?' does not work. Instead, questions like 'Do you like ice cream?', 'Have you ever met Brad Pitt?', 'Would you say yes if I asked you on a date?' or even the cheeky 'What is the opposite of no?' all work well.

The most important aspect of gameplay is to encourage inventiveness in the responses. You may wish to ban 'maybe', or only allow it once. You can also make a rule that players cannot repeat any responses, in order to encourage creative thinking.

The Aim of the Game

This surprisingly difficult game demands significant self-control and concentration. More importantly, however, it aims to get players to explore the wealth of possibilities within speech and dialogue. It can work as an effective prelude to playwriting exercises.

Players	Age	Time	Skills
Any number	6+	10	Awareness, Familiarity, Imagination

Colombian Hypnosis

A fun mirroring game that promotes focus, observation skills and teamwork in pairs, originating from the workshops of Augusto Boal.

How to Play

Ask the players to find a partner and move into a space, standing opposite each other. In each pair, one player, let's call her Natasha, is going to hypnotise the other, let's call him Rick. In order to do this, Natasha must hold up her right hand, palm out, about one foot away from Rick's face.

The principle is for players to 'hypnotise' their partner with their hand. Wherever Natasha moves her hand, Rick will follow, keeping his face at a constant distance from her hand. Natasha must begin by moving her hand slowly, exploring the space, gently moving side to side or up and down. Rick must allow himself to be guided completely by Natasha. Once the players are comfortable, Natasha can become more inventive, moving her hand through different levels, using different speeds and dynamics, in order to make Rick's movements interesting. Natasha should try and stay on the spot and explore the dynamics of the immediate space. This can often yield more inventive results than allowing the players simply to follow each other around the room. After a few minutes, swap over, so that both players get a chance to be hypnotiser/hypnotised.

The Aim of the Game

The aim is to promote an effective working relationship between the two players. If the hypnotiser moves too quickly, then the hypnotised will not be able to follow. In order to be successful, both players need to be sensitive to each other's needs. The physical component of this game can also act as an effective warm-up, as the players' movements become more inventive.

Players	Age	Time	Skills
Any, in pairs	6+	10	Awareness, Teamwork, Trust, Familiarity

FOCUS

Liar, Liar!

An exercise in feigning truthfulness, an interesting way to get to know people in your group and to encourage conviction in performance.

How to Play

Split the group into teams of four or five players. There must be at least two teams. Each team has ten minutes to prepare a series of very short stories (less than a minute each) or statements, one per player. Only one player's story can be true, the others must all be false. When the teams are ready, one team takes the stage, and the others become the audience. The team who is 'up' must tell their stories, one by one, to the listening audience. When all the stories are told, ask the audience to vote on which player they believe is telling the truth. They need to use their powers of observation to try and spot any signals that might give the liars away.

If playing this game with inexperienced players, you might suggest that they pick stories around a theme. They should start by talking amongst themselves to find out who has an unusual true story. Once they have found one, then they can begin creating their false stories. Sometimes the stories might be short statements, even a single line; e.g. 'Last week I met the Prime Minister.' Sometimes they can be thoughtful recollections of dramatic incidents, full of elaborate detail, which never really happened!

Before the players recount their stories, discuss the body language and vocal ticks associated with both truthfulness and lying. People who are trying to convince often use eye contact, emphasis, detail and repetition to make their audience believe them. We readily associate looking at the floor, fiddling and bumbling with lying. Clever groups might like to use this knowledge tactically to put the audience off the scent!

The Aim of the Game

The aim is for the audience to use their knowledge of body language, voice and diction to spot the liars. The game also provides an opportunity for the players who are 'up' to use their naturalistic acting skills to try and act with conviction. This is an excellent way of beginning a session on body language.

Alternatively, link this game to the notion of 'good acting' in the contemporary theatre, in which we judge actors by their ability to convince us with sincerity. You might like to use the term 'naturalism' and the ideas of Stanislavsky as a way to link this style of acting into the wider history of the theatre. How can the players use the skills from this game to help them achieve naturalism and conviction in their performances?

Players	Age	Time	Skills
8+	8+	15	*Awareness, Dynamism, Self-control, Storytelling*

Wink Murder

An exciting team game in which the detective must find the murderer (the winker) before everyone is dead!

How to Play

This is an adaptation of the traditional children's 'spot the murderer' game. This version requires additional acting skills, through asking the players to mime a social event and 'die' in the most dramatic way possible!

Ask the players to sit in a circle. Set the scene, explaining that you are all at a posh dinner party in a beautiful country mansion. Conversation has turned to recent events, most prominently the mysterious murders that have been taking place all round the village. But when will the murderer strike again?

Now begin the game. Choose a detective and send this player out of the room. Then choose someone in the circle to be the murderer. To play the easy version, simply point to your chosen murderer so that everyone in the circle knows who they are. For more experienced players, ask everyone to shut their eyes, then move around the outside of the circle and tap your chosen murderer on the head. This adds a little spice to the game, as the players will also have to work out who the murderer is.

Once you have chosen your murderer, ask the group to call out 'Detective, detective, there's been a murder!' The detective must enter and stand in the middle of the circle. The players then mime eating dinner, watched by the detective, until the murderer begins killing people! The murderer can kill any player (except the detective) by winking at them. When winked at, a player must die in the most dramatic and bloodcurdling way, and then stay still, dead on the floor.

The detective's role is to spot the winker before all the other players are dead. When he has guessed correctly, the murderer then becomes the detective.

Encourage the players to make their deaths as dramatic as possible. Their death mimes should make the method of their murder clear too; e.g. were they shot, hung, electrocuted, drowned, poisoned?

The Aim of the Game

The game demands careful observation skills on the part of the detective. As a drama game specifically, this game promotes confidence and imagination in asking the players to mime both the dinner-party scenario and their elaborate deaths. It takes a high level of concentration as players must mime eating dinner whilst watching out for the murderer.

Players	Age	Time	Skills
Any number	6+	10	Teamwork, Awareness, Mime

PART FIVE

TEAMWORK

Ring of Hands

A quick-fire focus game in which players have to use their hands alone to pass signals around a circle.

How to Play

Ask the group to sit in a circle on their knees. Everyone puts their left hand into the circle, forming a ring of hands. Then everyone puts their right hand on the far side of their right-hand neighbour's left hand, thus forming a more complete ring of hands, in which no player's two hands are adjacent.

The aim is to 'pass the slap'. Calling a direction (e.g. 'To my left'), the first player slaps their hand to the floor. The next hand along must then slap the floor, thus passing the slap around the circle. This takes more coordination than might be expected, as a player's two hands will not be next to each other.

Once players have mastered the art of passing the slap around the circle, you can start adding extra challenges. If a player makes a mistake, they must take that hand out of the ring. A player can change the direction of the slap by slapping the floor twice. All players therefore have to be extra alert, to avoid preempting the slap if it changes direction just before getting to them!

A further variation is to add the 'fist'. If a player bangs their fist to the floor, the slap skips over one hand, before continuing around the ring. You can add a 'point' to another hand on the other side of the circle in order to transfer it across the ring.

The Aim of the Game

This is a great warm-up game, promoting concentration and teamwork. You can add further variations after a few weeks when the players become more familiar with the game – a hand wave might indicate changing direction and skipping one person; a thumbs-up might indicate players have to stand and quickly swap places.

Players	Age	Time	Skills
8+	8+	10	*Focus, Quick Responses*

Wolf and Sheep

A quick team game requiring the group to work together to protect one of the 'fold'.

How to Play

Get the group to join hands in a circle, except for one player, the 'wolf', who must stand outside the circle. Everyone in the circle is 'the fold' and must not, at any point, let go of each other's hands. Choose one member of the circle to be the 'sheep'. The group has to protect the sheep from the wolf by moving as a circle, making sure the wolf stays as far away as possible from the sheep. The circle must not be broken and the wolf is not allowed inside. The circle is allowed to move across the space, and to rotate, as long as it never breaks. The wolf must tap the sheep on the head, shoulder or arm. If they do, the sheep becomes the wolf, and you pick a new sheep.

The Aim of the Game

Preventing the wolf from getting to the sheep requires real cooperation between all the members of the circle, so promotes teamwork skills. It can also be quite exhilarating and physical so it makes a good warm-up game.

TEAMWORK

Players	Age	Time	Skills
12+	6+	10	*Pacing, Focus, Awareness*

Tableaux

A competitive team game in which groups must work together to produce images and scenes. An easy game to adapt to a themed or issue-based workshop.

How to Play

Split the group into teams of at least four players, ten is the maximum. You can play with any number of teams. Explain that you are going to give them a range of tableaux (frozen 3D pictures) to make. They might be objects, animals, pictures or representations of themes or feelings. Each team must use everyone in their group to create each tableau, and they are not allowed any props or furniture – just their bodies.

Call out '10 counts to make a... bridge!' Then count down aloud from 10, before calling 'Freeze!' On hearing this, each team must stop moving and hold their tableau. Award a point to the best team, giving credit for inventiveness and originality. You may choose to ask each team to show their tableau in turn, and ask for positive comments from other groups. Once a winner for that round has been decided, continue the game with the next subject.

One of the greatest assets of this game is its flexibility to suit any age group. For younger players, begin by asking for simple shapes; e.g. a square, a straight line, or a box. Then challenge them by asking for animals or objects; e.g. a lion, a monster.

For older players, challenge them to use practical logic; e.g. a bridge, an equilateral triangle. You could encourage them to create scenic pictures; e.g. a circus tent, an airport lounge. You might like to remember these scenes as starting points for improvisations later in the session.

You can also theme this activity to explore specific issues or ideas in a play. Choose images that relate to your theme; if you are exploring racism, for instance, ask for an image of prejudice and an image of unity. Alternatively, use this as a starting point for generating ideas about the world of the play; ask for images of the Capulet's house or Juliet's balcony in *Romeo and Juliet*.

The Aim of the Game

The key challenge is teamwork and innovation. Some players inevitably attempt to direct their groups. However, it quickly becomes obvious that cooperation as a team is the key to success. Groups will achieve most when they listen to each other, act fast and follow their initial ideas. Discourage groups from copying one another by giving credit for originality.

Variations and Extensions

To develop this game, you may ask the teams to bring their tableaux to life. This works particularly well with the scenic pictures, as each different character can come to life; the more animated their performances, the better.

Players	Age	Time	Skills
8+	6+	15	*Imagination, Pacing, Spontaneity*

1, 2, 3, Washing Machine!

An energetic and silly game that requires players to work together to mime various objects.

How to Play

Begin by explaining the four 'objects' involved in this game, and how to make them. Each object requires three players.

Washing machine

Two players stand as far away from each other as they comfortably can, turn back to back and hold hands. The third player stands in between them and moves their arms round in circles to suggest the action of a washing machine. All the players make washing-machine sloshing noises.

Toaster

Two players hold hands at shoulder height, facing each other. The third player crouches in between, and then jumps up, at which point all three say 'Bing!' as the toast pops up.

Sports car

Two players on the outside, miming the wheels, and the player in the middle jigging up and down 'steering', whilst all three make revving noises.

Television

The two outside players stand apart, facing the front, with their outside arms by their sides and their inside arms touching at shoulder height, bridging the gap. This time the person in the middle has to dance about as if on MTV (or a station of their choice) whilst all three create the musical backing.

Once everyone is familiar with all four objects, the game can begin. Ask all the players to stand in a circle. You stand in the middle, count from 1 to 3 and then point at a player and call out one of the three objects. That player, with the person on either side of them (i.e. so three people are involved), have to immediately respond as the object, the person you pointed at forming the middle player in each creation. As soon as they are doing so, you begin again: '1, 2, 3…' and choose another of the objects, selecting a new player to point at. The faster you move on, the more difficult it becomes. As players become familiar with the game, you can even point to more than one person at once and create spontaneous electrical appliances all around the circle! You might also like to be inventive with your objects, creating new ones, or asking the group to create them as a warm-up exercise before the game begins.

The Aim of the Game

The aim is for the players to act quickly and remember the details of each machine they are trying to make, which requires both memory skills and excellent teamwork!

Players	Age	Time	Skills
8+	**6+**	**15**	*Energy, Focus, Memory*

Picture Postcards

A creative team game in which groups have to create physical postcards of places in the world, using themselves as the subjects, for the other teams to guess.

How to Play

Divide the group into teams of a minimum of three, ideally more. Explain, in character, that you are Great Aunt Elfrida, or Great Uncle Tom, and that you are so pleased to have returned home after many years of traveling around the world! No wonder none of the group recognised you! On your travels you collected postcards in every country you visited, and you are now going to share them with the group.

However, on the last leg of the voyage, your suitcase fell off the boat and filled up with water! Thankfully it was rescued by one of the bright, young sailors, who dived in and retrieved it for you. But unfortunately, the sea washed all the writing off the back of the postcards, so you can't remember which countries they were from. You would be very grateful if everyone could help you work out where you visited, as your memory is starting to go a little – it must be too much sun after all your tropical adventures!

Now, give each team five minutes working together to create a postcard of somewhere in the world that Great Aunt Elfrida or Great Uncle Tom might have visited. They need to use everyone in their group to form the postcard as a frozen tableau, which they create using their own bodies. Get them to brainstorm the images you are likely to see on a postcard; famous landmarks, local dancing, activities, people eating local foods, the scenery, etc. Countries which often work well in this game include France, Germany, Spain, Italy, Egypt, America, Australia, China and India, but do encourage older players to be as innovative as possible.

When they have created their postcard, they show it to the rest of the group, who must guess which country it represents.

The Aim of the Game

This game promotes teamwork, but it also gives groups an opportunity to share their knowledge of the world. If you are working with a multiracial group, this can be an interesting means of allowing people to share a little of their own culture with the rest of the group.

Variations and Extensions

Team members could improvise a short monologue of what was written on back of the postcard. This could serve as a hint if the others have trouble guessing, or could be the beginning of a longer improvisation about Great Aunt Elfrida's travels.

Players	Age	Time	Skills
6+	8+	10	*Imagination*

Star Wars

A very popular team game, especially with younger players, in which two competing groups have to react simultaneously to battling Jedi Knights.

How to Play

Split the group into two teams, the 'Jedi Knights' and 'Stormtroopers'. Choose a leader for each team. The two teams must stand facing each other, with their leaders slightly in front of the teams, directly facing the other leader. Each leader takes it in turn to make three moves to attack the other team. The challenge is for the team to react together, as one, to avoid attack.

The two leaders hold their imaginary swords in front of them, and take it in turns to mime an attack on the other team. As the leader makes each attacking move, the opposition team must move together to avoid the attack. The whole game must happen in slow motion. There are three basic moves, which can be played in any order.

Firstly, the leader can swing the imaginary sword low to the ground, as if trying to slice off the opposition's ankles. When he does this, the opposing team must jump up off the ground, as if avoiding the sword.

Secondly, he can swoop the sword down in an arc, from high to low, either from right to left or left to right. When he does so, the opposing team must jump one pace in the opposite direction, as if avoiding the sword.

Thirdly, he can swing his sword as if trying to cut off the heads of the opposing team. When he does this, the opposing team must duck immediately.

If any of the team members make a mistake, or are too slow, they are killed by the imaginary sword, and join the opposing team.

Do ensure that the speed is closely regulated, so as not to become too fast and lose focus. The aim is to encourage precision, hence the slow-motion nature of the combat. Once players are familiar with the moves, encourage them to be imaginative – ask the players to collaboratively invent new moves in order to spice the game up.

The Aim of the Game

The challenge of the game is for each team to react as one to the mimed attack of the opposing leader. This game promotes teamwork and precision, and is a good starting point for any work on choruses and group scenes.

Variations and Extensions

This game can easily be adapted to an alternative battle theme, depending on the age and interests of your group. Harry Potter's Gryffindor team against the slinky Slytherin players often works well.

Alternatively, you can explore the idea of a Greek chorus, who move and speak in unison, using appropriate movements to explore the basics of choral performance.

Players	Age	Time	Skills
10+	10+	10	Coordination, Precision, Quick Responses

TEAMWORK

Enigma

An exciting team game in which the group must pass a secret 'code' between each other without the code breaker cracking it first!

How to Play

In this game, the 'code breaker' has to identify who has the 'code' by spotting a signal passed between players.

Ask the players to stand in a circle. Everyone must choose a personal gesture and show it to the group. Subtle gestures tend to work best at first; e.g. tugging your ear, rubbing your nose, winking or adjusting your trousers. However, practised players may choose more brazen motions to make gameplay more challenging.

When everyone has chosen a gesture, choose a code breaker and ask them to wait outside the room. Now choose someone to start with the 'code', let's call her Annie. Then ask the code breaker to come back in.

The code breaker must stand in the middle of the circle and try and spot the code being passed. Annie waits for an opportune moment to pass the code on to a player of her choice, let's call him Paul. She does this by using her gesture. Annie's gesture is rubbing her nose. Annie rubs her nose at Paul, then Paul rubs his nose back to show that he accepts the code from Annie. He then has the code until he sees a good moment to pass it to someone else and they accept it. He passes the code on by doing his gesture (pushing his hair behind his ear) at Dan, who then repeats the gesture to accept it from Paul. When the code breaker guesses correctly (only allow three lives), the person who is caught with the code becomes the detective.

The Aim of the Game

In working together to keep the code secret from the code breaker, the game demands discretion, observation and teamwork. The secretive, spying nature of the game is always popular with young players.

Variations and Extensions

If you and your actors are ambitious, try the following suggestion to make the game even more challenging! Set the game up as usual, but when the code breaker arrives, the other players move around the room rather than standing still in the circle. If they are moving and gesturing a little it becomes much more difficult for the code breaker to spot the real code being passed.

Players	Age	Time	Skills
Any number	8+	10	Movement, Energy, Focus

Doctor, Doctor!

A game of logic, skill and flexibility, in which the doctor has to solve the riddle of the tangled team!

How to Play

Choose a player to be the doctor, and ask them to face the wall until you are ready. The others are all the patients, and begin by joining hands in a circle. Then, give them one minute to 'tangle themselves up', stepping over and under each other's arms, crawling through legs and spinning around until they cannot tangle themselves any more. The only rule is that, during this process, they must not let go of each other's hands!

Then, when one minute is up, the group call out 'Doctor, doctor!' The doctor's job is then to untangle the players, again without breaking the hand-holds. If the players have kept hold of each other's hands it should be possible to untangle them. Whatever the outcome, this game is always the source of great fun and hilarity with every age group.

The Aim of the Game

As well as being a great source of amusement, this game teaches the group to be patient with each other and to support one player in their mission to help everyone else out of a physical dilemma.

Players	Age	Time	Skills
8+	8+	10	*Logic, Movement, Focus, Familiarity*

PART SIX

TRUST

Friendly Follower

A three-stage trust game that builds a feeling of confidence between partners.

How to Play

Ask everyone to find a partner, let's call ours Esme and Ali. There are several stages of the game, each of which builds on the last to demand a higher level of trust between partners.

For the first task, Esme must close her eyes and let Ali take her hand. Ali's task is then to lead Esme around the room very slowly, ensuring that Esme is safe and does not bump into anything or anyone else. After several minutes ask them to swap over and repeat the exercise.

For the second task, repeat the first activity but instead of holding hands, Esme's only contact with Ali is fingertip to fingertip (ask them to use their index finger only). Ali must walk slowly enough that Esme can follow safely without losing contact between their fingertips. Then ask them to swap over.

The third part of the game is the most challenging. Hopefully, by this point, the partners will have begun to trust each other. This time there is no physical contact between them. Esme must lead Ali purely by the sound of her voice. She needs to give clear vocal instructions and maintain a constant stream of words, either commands or encouragement, in order to make sure Ali knows where she is at all times. Esme must pay particular attention to other players leading their partners about in the same space. Ali needs to listen extremely carefully for the sound of Esme's voice and ignore the other voices giving instructions.

The Aim of the Game

The aim is to build trust within each pair. This is a useful game for the early stages of rehearsal, when people do not know each other very well, as it helps to forge partnerships and friendships amongst strangers.

Variations and Extensions

Some facilitators choose to make the game more challenging by setting chairs through the space as obstacles. If playing with a relatively large group (say fourteen or more), then the other players are usually obstacle enough, but you may wish to adapt the game to suit your own situation.

> **Warning:** It is imperative that this game is carefully supervised and played with mature players only. It is inadvisable to play it with a very large group, as you may be unable to monitor the players closely enough to ensure the safety of every individual.

Players	Age	Time	Skills
Any, in pairs	10+	10	Awareness, Teamwork, Familiarity

Leap of Faith

The ultimate trust game where players allow themselves to be caught mid-air by the group.

How to Play

Ask for a volunteer to be the jumper. The ultimate aim is for this player to run towards the group from the other end of the room, and be caught on the supportive 'landing pad' that is formed by the arms of the rest of the team. This takes a good deal of trust from the jumper, reliability from the group and careful supervision.

In order to do this exercise safely, the catching group needs to consist of a minimum of eight people. They need to form into two lines facing each other, and each join hands with someone on the opposite side, to form a landing pad. Ensure that they do not stand too rigidly; they will need to bend their knees slightly to absorb the weight of the jumper. You must also ensure that they are far enough away from any walls that, if the jumper overshoots, there is no possibility of crashing into a wall.

As in every trust game, the level of difficulty must be built up slowly. Firstly, ask the jumper to stand next to the landing pad, facing away from it, and gently fall backwards onto it. At this stage the pairs forming the landing pad should position themselves in order to create a wall for the jumper to lean or fall back onto. This requires some pairs to go low down and other to stagger the level of their arms accordingly. To ensure that the group can easily bear the jumper's weight, try this a few times.

Then ask the jumper to turn around to face the group, and to gently dive onto the landing pad from a foot away. The jumper must hold their arms out in front of them, above their head, as though diving into a pool, to ensure that his or her elbows and hands are out of the way. The others forming the landing pad should position their arms like a bed, standing in two rows facing each other so that their arms create a solid platform.

Once the jumper is confident diving onto the landing pad whilst standing next to it, ask them to take a couple of steps away, and then slowly jog towards it, before diving on. You can continue to increase the distance until the jumper is comfortable running from the other side of the room.

The Aim of the Game

The aim is to achieve trust between each individual and the rest of the group. Explain the importance of supportiveness within a class or theatre ensemble. This exercise helps to build a bond between members of the group, and is an effective game to use at the beginning of a series of workshops, production or project.

> **Warning:** It is imperative that this game is carefully supervised and played with mature players only. It is inadvisable to play it with a very large group, as you may be unable to monitor the players closely enough to ensure the safety of every individual.

Players	Age	Time	Skills
12+	16+	15	Teamwork, Familiarity, Focus

Falling Trees

A team-building trust game in which players gain the confidence to 'fall' into the safety of the group.

How to Play

Ask the players to make teams of between six and nine people. Choose one player, let's call her Peggy, to stand in the middle. The rest of her group must form a tight circle around her. All of the players must be touching side to side, to ensure there are no gaps in the circle. They put their hands up, palms facing towards Peggy, to form a protective barrier, lightly touching her. Peggy stands in the centre with her arms up against her chest and her eyes closed. Then she can gently start to 'fall'. The group around her are responsible for catching her and gently pushing her back and forth, as she falls from side to side. For this to work she needs to try and keep her body as straight as possible, and to relax. They will gain her trust, and as they do, she will undoubtedly relax to the point when she is reliant on them completely. Ensure everyone has the opportunity to be the 'falling tree'.

The Aim of the Game

The aim is to build trust within the group, and to encourage each individual to allow themselves to rely totally on their team. There will certainly be some players who are nervous of this game at first. If you are playing this with a new group, you might like to repeat it several sessions later and observe how much more trusting the players are of each other after they become used to working together.

> **Warning:** It is imperative that this game is carefully supervised and played with mature players only. It is inadvisable to play it with a very large group, as you may be unable to monitor the players closely enough to ensure the safety of every individual.

Players	Age	Time	Skills
6+	**12+**	**10**	*Teamwork, Familiarity, Focus*

PART SEVEN

CHARACTER

Introducing
Characterisation

Family Portraits

A quick team game in which groups spontaneously create family portraits of all manner of weird and wonderful families.

How to Play

The idea of the game is to create snapshots of various 'character families' at high speed. Split the group into teams of a minimum of four people, ideally more. The teams line up, one team behind the other, facing the playing space. The game begins as the leader shouts out 'a family of... firefighters' or other random group that takes your fancy (see below for some ideas). As soon as they hear this instruction: the team at the front of the line runs into the space and makes a 'family portrait' pose as these characters. Then you shout the next instruction: 'a family of killer ants', for instance. Immediately, the team in the space break their pose and run to the back of the line, whilst the next team runs forward, posing as a menacing family of killer ants.

Almost any group of characters works for this game. You can suggest families of animals (birds, jungle creatures, fish, cats, rabbits), professionals (doctors, firemen, pop stars, school teachers, footballers), fictional characters (elves, gargoyles, Muppets, Greek gods) or inanimate objects (plants, cutlery, ballgowns). Encourage the players to consider the different people who appear in a family photograph (the proud father, the naughty kid, the elderly relative, the harassed mother, the glamorous auntie, the distracted uncle). The various ages and personalities of the characters should be apparent in the frozen poses.

The Aim of the Game

The game aims to get each team working together in a fast and spontaneous way. It promotes imagination and also gives players a chance to think about many varied characters, which, depending on your plans for the rest of the session, could be drawn on as inspiration in later exercises.

Variations and Extensions

Once the game has got going, I often like to call two groups up simultaneously. If you choose to do this, give them two related families; 'a family of carnivores' and 'a family of vegetarians', for example, or 'a family of chickens' and 'a family of foxes'. The two groups must create their portraits facing each other and often the relationship between the two is a great source of comedy!

You can also use this game to explore characters in a text. If exploring Shakespeare's *Macbeth*, for instance, try calling out 'the Macbeth family' or 'the witches' for an engaging way to explore the characters' backgrounds away from the text.

Players	Age	Time	Skills
8+	8+	10	*Teamwork, Imagination, Pacing*

Lead With Your...

A humorous physicalisation game, based on Commedia dell'Arte *techniques, which works both as a fun warm-up and as a platform for developing characters.*

How to Play

Ask the players to find a space. Explain that many 'stock characters' (standard, recognisable characters such as 'the hero' or 'the villain') in drama have recognisable ways of moving because they 'lead' with specific parts of their body. The leading body part often corresponds with the character's objectives; e.g. the greedy old man leads with his belly. Then begin the game. Suggest a body part – e.g. the nose – and ask the players to move around the space silently, with their nose leading the way. Explain that their noses must not only go first, but must make the decisions about where to go. Where does the nose want to go? What can it smell? The rest of the body must follow afterwards. After everyone has had a chance to try leading with their noses, pick out a couple of successful players to watch as an example. Ask the others to suggest what kind of characters they see emerging; e.g. a nosey old woman. Then try out a new body part: chin, elbows, chest, pelvis, knees...

The Aim of the Game

The game encourages physical experimentation and an awareness of the link between body and character. It is a great jumping-off point for characterisation, and you may wish to set up improvisations later in the session with the characters who have been devised in this game.

Variations and Extensions

Leading with certain body parts is a significant feature of characterisation in the *Commedia dell'Arte* tradition. Investigating this genre further will reveal many similar exercises, and expose your players to a rich and dynamic form of theatre.

Players	Age	Time	Skills
Any number	6+	15	Movement, Imagination, Focus

Themed Musical Chairs

A favourite amongst younger players, this game involves a mixture of characterisation, musicality and energy.

How to Play

This is a very simple adaptation of the popular children's game. Place one less chair than the number of players around the room. Choose a themed piece of music and get the players to brainstorm associated characters; e.g. if using music from Disney's *The Lion King*, characters might include lions, hyenas, parrots and monkeys. Ask the players to think about the speed of their characters, their facial expressions and their way of moving.

Decide on a character for the first round, then play the music. Players must move around the room as that character, using their entire bodies. When the music stops, they run to the nearest chair and sit down. The player without a chair is out, and chooses the next character.

The Aim of the Game

The game encourages players to develop speedy reactions, mime and listening skills, whilst creating each character effectively.

Variations and Extensions

Good themed music to choose includes:

Spies
  James Bond or *Mission Impossible*

Underwater
  'Under the Sea' from Disney's *The Little Mermaid*

Jungle
  Any songs from Disney's *The Jungle Book*

Harry Potter
  Music from the film score is evocative and atmospheric

+ Recorded music			
Players	**Age**	**Time**	**Skills**
6+	6+	10	*Teamwork, Imagination, Pacing*

Grandma's Hat

An imaginative version of Grandmother's Footsteps, *involving items of costume as characterisation tools.*

How to Play

Choose one player to be 'Grandma', and send them to one end of the room, facing the wall. Ask the other players to stand against the opposite wall. Scatter the hats around on the floor, so that they all lie between Grandma and the players.

When you say 'Go!', the players must begin to sneak towards Grandma. Their aim is to get to Grandma without her seeing them move. Every so often she will whip around to face them, in an attempt to catch them moving. At this point, they must freeze immediately in their exact position. If she sees anyone move, she sends them back to the wall again. The first player to touch Grandma wins, and takes her place in the next round.

Whilst they move towards Grandma, each player chooses a hat to put on, so they must travel to the hat first. As soon as they put it on their heads, they have to continue their walk towards Grandma in the style of the hat-wearer. It may be a posh lady's hat, in which case they should tiptoe genteelly across the floor, or a soldier's hat, which would require the wearer to march the rest of the way. This makes the game far more challenging!

The Aim of the Game

The basic aim is to teach self-control, as the players must avoid being caught by controlling their movements. However, this particular dramatic version also gives players the opportunity to mime a variety of characters, and to think about the link between character and costume.

+ Assorted hats or other pieces of costume			
Players	**Age**	**Time**	**Skills**
Any number	**6+**	**10**	*Imagination, Self-control*

The Ministry of Funny Walks

An amusing characterisation and warm-up game, based on the sketch from Monty Python, in which players have to amuse each other with the most outlandish ways of walking they can think of.

How to Play

Ask the players to stand in a circle. Choose someone to start, let's call her Colleen.

Very simply, Colleen decides on a funny way of travelling across the circle, moving first to the middle, then pausing, looking around, choosing a 'target' (Emma) then approaching Emma to swap places with her. Colleen then takes Emma's place. Emma chooses a new funny walk, moves to the centre of the circle, before heading towards a new player whose turn it will be next.

Encourage the players to explore every conceivable way of travelling across the circle, using varying paces, height levels, dynamics, leading with different parts of their bodies, crossing the floor on a body part other than their feet. The range of characters that quickly develop with the spontaneous nature of this game is equally funny and astounding.

The Aim of the Game

The game encourages individual players to think creatively about characterisation and movement.

Players	Age	Time	Skills
6+	6+	10	*Energy, Movement, Imagination*

Emotion Machines

A dynamic game that requires the group to create a human machine representing a feeling; an effective starting point for exploring emotions.

How to Play

Divide the group into teams of six or more. Allocate each team an emotion. Everyone within the team must choose a sound or phrase that relates to the feeling. They must then choose an appropriate action to accompany their sound.

Now they can begin to build their machine. Each person's action and phrase needs to act like a cog of the machine. Each will be prompted physically by someone else's action, and in turn, will prompt another player's reaction.

One person begins by going into the space and performing their sound and action, repeating it continuously. The next player then joins the first, building their own action onto the existing machine, so that one action prompts another to begin.

For instance, let us imagine we are building a 'Happiness Machine'. Richard goes first. His action is to jump in the air, saying 'Yes, I won!' He goes into the space and begins to do this repeatedly. Hannah must now add herself onto Richard's movement. Her action is a sway from side to side, saying 'I'm so in love!' Now, in order to link to his action, she has to choose an appropriate way to perform hers so that it can be prompted by his. So, when he lands, she decides, his landing will prompt her sway to begin. She moves into the space and does just that. Then Ollie joins on to Hannah's movement. His chosen movement was a hug gesture, whilst saying 'Thanks for the present!' Now, when Hannah sways sideways, Ollie hugs her and says 'Thanks for the present!' before she sways back. The others then add themselves on, and the machine builds until everyone is incorporated.

To add further details, ask the players to work out the start-up and shutdown sequences for their machines. How does the machine turn on? Does it shudder? Does it make strange noises? Do all the wheels and cogs begin at the same time or one by one?

Once they have practised their machines, ask each team to perform their sequence. You might like the other teams to guess which emotion each machine represents.

The Aim of the Game

The aim is for the group to work together to produce a cohesive, rhythmic, dynamic machine. Whilst the exercise promotes teamwork, it also provides an opportunity to think about the nuances of a single emotion, and to experiment with portraying it in its many and varied forms.

Variations and Extensions

You can use machines to explore all manner of concepts and scenarios other than emotions. You can build a location machine (often amusing for younger players), creating a farmyard or a space machine, for instance.

As a challenge for older players, you might like to ask them to create a machine based on a period, style of theatre, play titles, or even a practitioner. This can be an enjoyable revision exercise for students of theatre; particular examples might include a 'Brecht Machine', 'Greek Tragedy Machine' or 'Dada Machine'.

Players	Age	Time	Skills
6+	8+	10	Teamwork, Imagination, Precision

Psychiatrist

A teamwork improvisation game in which a psychiatrist has to diagnose the group's problem.

How to Play

Ask the players to sit in a circle. Choose one person to be the 'psychiatrist', and send them out of the room. The remaining players then decide on a rule to give themselves a new identity. For example:

Easy Rules

> Everyone is from a certain country.
>
> Everyone has a specific job; e.g. jockeys or scuba-divers (the more unusual the better).
>
> Everyone must begin their answers with the letter B (or other letter of your choice).

Medium Rules

> Everyone becomes the person sitting on their left.
>
> Everyone is from a particular play/TV show/film (establish characters before you begin).

Difficult Rules

> Everyone has a phobia of a certain letter or word, and reacts every time this is said.
>
> All the girls in the group are tour guides and all the boys are bus drivers (or some other alternatives that create two contrasting identities).

Once you have agreed on a rule, invite the psychiatrist back in. The psychiatrist must then diagnose the group's problem (the rule) by asking the players questions. A perceptive psychiatrist will soon focus their questions in the right direction:

> STEVE (*the psychiatrist*): What is your name?
>
> ALI: Marie.
>
> STEVE: What is your name?
>
> LINDSEY: Genevieve.
>
> STEVE: What about you, what's your name?
>
> DAN: Jean-Claude.
>
> STEVE: You, next to Jean-Claude, what are you having for lunch?

TIM: Baguettes with *fromage*. Maybe with snails too.

STEVE: Are you all French?

ALL: YES!

If a player notices that another player answers incorrectly, the observant player shouts 'Psychiatrist!' and everyone has to swap places, reforming the circle before continuing play. Play until the psychiatrist has reached a correct diagnosis, and then choose a new psychiatrist.

The Aim of the Game

The game requires high levels of observation from the psychiatrist, and spontaneity and intelligence from the other players.

Variations and Extensions

With highly competent groups of small numbers, you can give each player a different identity, which the psychiatrist then has to guess (a familiar character or personality).

Players	Age	Time	Skills
6+	**10+**	**15**	*Awareness, Teamwork, Spontaneity*

Object Puppetry Challenge

A game that requires players to create a character for an inanimate object, and to learn basic puppetry skills.

How to Play

This simple exercise can be extremely rewarding, and it is worth allowing adequate time for the players to be as inventive and experimental as possible.

Begin the exercise by explaining that characters do not have to be human, or even animal – a character is any being that has a personality. Actors sometimes have to play an object that has a mind of its own, whereas in real life it does not, such as trees in a haunted wood as they come to life. Encourage the group to consider moments in stories or films when it seems inanimate objects might be alive; e.g. the statue in *The Happy Prince*, the car in *Chitty Chitty Bang Bang* and the kitchen implements in Disney's *Beauty and the Beast*.

Then explain that you have a bag of characters who are all waiting to be let out. Hand the objects out to the players. Then ask each player to find a space with their object, and give them five minutes to find its character. Begin by asking them to look at the object carefully. Try and take notice of every detail, the colours, texture, moving parts, weight, and sounds. How might these attributes relate to a personality?

Then ask them to think about the purpose of the object, and consider how that purpose relates to the character. A pair of scissors might be a scary character with a sharp mouth. A fluffy ball, in contrast, is likely to have a much softer personality.

Ask the players to look for the features that we identify with a character – eyes, nose, mouth, arms, legs, etc. Does their object have any of these? The pair of scissors clearly has a mouth (the blades) and potentially two eyes (the finger holes). The hard cover of a book might become wings or legs. Then give the group several minutes to create a simple improvisation for their character, as simple as it walking in and out of a space.

Share these improvisations with the group and comment on what makes a successful puppet animation. To extend the activity, you may wish to ask them to work in pairs and create a short interactive scenario between the two puppets. The results are often incredibly creative and quite beautiful. Watching a teabag character commit suicide by throwing himself into the cup of boiling water was a really stunning miniature piece of theatre, performed in a canteen! Sometimes the simplest ideas are the most effective.

The Aim of the Game

The game allows players to think about character in the broadest form, to stretch their imaginations and to become familiar with basic puppetry.

+ Assorted random objects			
Players	**Age**	**Time**	**Skills**
Any, in pairs	6+	15	Mime, Improvisation, Precision, Imagination

Character Development

Pauper to Prince

A competitive game that encourages players to explore the presentation of status through frozen poses.

How to Play

This game works best when prefaced with a short discussion about the meaning of 'status', and its importance in characterisation. Explain that a character's status can be affected by a number of factors, including wealth, age, social position, knowledge, profession, confidence, the views of their peers (think about a gang leader), experience, gender, race, etc.

On stage, we often see a character's status level fluctuate depending on circumstances and audience. Hamlet, for instance, acts high status when confronting his enemies, yet he is low status when he sees the ghost of his father. The actor will need to vary his body language in order to reveal the difference between the confident, high-status Prince and the humility of the scared son. Generally, high-status characters take up more space, occupy superior stage positions (raised up or further upstage), and use eye contact and bolder gestures. However, there are interesting exceptions, which can be explored in this game.

Ask the players to line up along one side of the playing space. The first player then goes into the space and takes the lowest-status position they can think of, freezing there. Encourage attention to body language, gesture, facial expression and eye contact to communicate their status to the audience.

Now ask the next player in line to come in and take a position that is slightly higher status than the first. Often the two positions will relate to each other; e.g. if the first actor is a humble, shrunken man begging for food, the second might become a beggar with a tiny morsel to eat. Once the second actor has chosen his pose, ask the others to confirm who appears to be higher status and why. If necessary, ask the second actor to adapt his position until it is agreed that he is highest. The first player may then 'unfreeze' and join the back of the line. The next player then enters the space and takes a position slightly higher status than the current player's, and so on and so forth, until they get stuck.

At this point, encourage the players to think laterally. How can someone undermine the grand physical size of the high-status actor? What activity can they mime to give themselves higher status? Ideas might include putting an imaginary gun to the other's head, pretending to direct them in a play, or pulling a face behind their backs, all of which give the new player higher status than the person who appears initially to have the highest status in the scene.

The Aim of the Game

To encourage players to explore the idea of status, firstly from a physical perspective, but then, as the game progresses, to consider other factors that can be brought into play.

Players	Age	Time	Skills
6+	10+	15	*Imagination, Awareness, Status*

Aces High!

*A guessing game using improvisation and playing cards
to allocate status in a scene.*

How to Play

There are two parts to this game. Begin by splitting
the group in half; half take the stage, the others
become the audience. Choose a scenario in which
people of varied status levels might mingle; e.g. at a
cocktail party, on a railway platform or in a
nightclub.

For the first part of the game, give each player a
playing card. The number on the card dictates
status level: ace being the highest, 2 is lowest. They
must look at their card, and then put it in their
pocket, making sure no one else sees. Then start
the scene. The actors must play a character
according to their given status. Encourage them to
use body language, to choose an appropriate job, to
consider who they would want to speak to and
how they might feel. Give the scene a little time to
get going, so that the audience has had a chance to
observe each of the players. Then pause the scene.

Now ask the audience to suggest where, in a line
from lowest (on the left) to highest (on the right),
each of the players should stand. Once the
audience has debated the position of each player,
ask them to reveal their cards one by one.
Depending on how accurate the guesses are, take
this opportunity to discuss which factors helped to
identify status. Then swap the groups, giving the
new actors a different scenario. Encourage them to
use their observations from the first round to help
them reveal their status accurately.

For the second part of the game, the players are
allocated cards again but this time they must not
look at them. Instead they wear the cards on their
foreheads. They can either lick the back of the card
and stick it to their foreheads (which works best
but gets expensive if you buy new cards every
time!), or hold it up with one finger. Provide a
scenario, as before. This time the actors must focus
on reacting to other people's status. They must
then work out their own status level, according to

their treatment in the scene. After several minutes, ask the actors to get into a line according to the status they think they are. Ask them to guess one by one. Was this easier or harder? Take this opportunity to emphasise the importance of reactions in determining status for an audience.

Watch out for characters trying to spot their cards reflected in other players' glasses! You might like to ask those wearing glasses to take them off if they can.

The Aim of the Game

This game is an effective way of encouraging the actors to think about status both from an active and reactive position. It is also an excellent exercise in observation skills.

+ Deck of playing cards			
Players	**Age**	**Time**	**Skills**
12+	8+	15	*Imagination, Precision, Status, Improvisation*

Slingshot

A quick-fire emotion game that gets players to explore the wealth of possible interpretations of a single phrase.

How to Play

Ask the players to get into two lines, A and B, facing each other. Choose a player from line A to begin, let's call him Neal. He points at someone in line B (Claire) and improvises a one-line comment to her; e.g. 'I love your shoes.' Claire then responds with a one-line answer; e.g. 'They are size eight.'

Neal then takes one step towards Claire and repeats his statement, this time using a different emotion. 'I love your shoes,' he says sulkily, as if he was jealous that she has nice warm feet. She then takes a step towards him, adapting her reply to suit his. 'They are size eight,' she gloats smugly.

Neal then takes another step towards her and changes his emotion again. 'I love your shoes,' he shouts angrily. She steps forward humbly. 'They're size eight,' she replies, wincing, as if she has been told off.

They continue to move towards each other, changing the emotion each time, passing each other in the middle, and continuing until they reach the other person's place in the line. When they are close together in the middle, they may find angry or loving tones; when they have just passed each other, their responses may become lonesome or wistful. This may be an interesting point for discussion once all players have completed the game. Encourage players to work against their assumed convictions – what happens if you try angry tones when you are back to back, or loving tones from a distance? Sometimes these ideas prove the most engaging and enlightening.

Once the pair are back in the line, choose another player to begin.

The Aim of the Game

The game explores the multiple interpretative possibilities within any given dialogue, and to investigate the effect of relative distances on emotion. Within the game, the actors are asked to move towards and away from each other in order to feel the effect of proximity on their emotional responses.

Variations and Extensions

You can adapt this game to help actors explore their roles in a play. Ask them to choose a line from their script, and work with a partner who they speak to in a scene. Play the game with the actors using their lines, in order to explore a wide range of ways of delivering them. Sometimes they might find fresh and original ideas that help them in their final performances.

Players	Age	Time	Skills
Any, in pairs	10+	10	Imagination, Confidence

Max's Motivations

A game to help actors explore the strength of their objectives in a given scenario, as often used by Max Stafford-Clark in his rehearsals.

How to Play

Pick two volunteers. Give them a simple dramatic scenario in which both have a clear objective (i.e. something they want). For instance, Dave and Becky have found a wallet on the pavement. Dave wants to hand it in to the police station. Becky wants to keep it because there is £100 inside.

Take the aces and face cards out of the deck in advance, so the cards available are 2 to 10. 10 is the strongest objective, so a player with this card will do whatever it takes to achieve their goal. 2 is the weakest objective level, so a player with this card is almost totally passive, they almost couldn't care less... but not quite (they still must play their objective, albeit lazily).

Ask each player to pick a card at random, look at it, and then put it in their pocket. They must not show it to each other or to the audience. Then the two actors perform their scene, playing the strength of their objective according to their card.

The conclusion of the scene will depend on the cards drawn. If Becky had a 2 and Dave a 10, they would end up taking the wallet straight to the police station, as Dave wants, with little discussion. If Dave had a 5 and Becky an 8, he would put up a bit of a fight but then agree to keep the wallet. If both characters have a mid-range card, the scene is likely to be more difficult to bring to a close! The actors must find a way of bringing it to a conclusion, at which point the audience has to guess which number each actor has.

The Aim of the Game

The game helps explore the importance of objectives, or desires, within a scene. Varying the strength of the characters' objectives will allow actors to find a range of possibilities within any given scenario. The principles of this exercise can easily be applied during rehearsal to any given scene, in order to find vital dynamics and increase the dramatic potency of the situation.

The same principle can be used to experiment with other variables within a scene too, in order to bring spontaneity to a rehearsal and to add detail to a scene. For instance, Max Stafford-Clark used this exercise during rehearsals for *The Overwhelming* by JT Rogers (National Theatre/Out of Joint, 2006). He used cards to determine the drunkenness of two characters in a bar scene. After trying several different card combinations (9 and 9 – both very drunk; 8 and 2 – one drunk, one sober; 4 and 7 – one tipsy, one quite intoxicated), he arrived at a dynamic but believable decision, which added conviction and charisma to the scene.

+ Deck of playing cards			
Players	**Age**	**Time**	**Skills**
4+ in pairs	10+	15	*Imagination, Precision, Status*

Character Hotseat

*An improvisational activity in which characters are
interviewed and investigated.*

How to Play

This is an ideal game to use if the group is
rehearsing or studying a specific text, or if preparing
monologues for a performance or examination.

Set a chair in the performance space and ask the
players to sit as an audience facing the chair. Then
choose someone to be 'up'. Ask them to select a
character from the play; their own character, of
course, if they are working towards a
performance.

Then introduce the setting for the interview,
choosing somewhere appropriate depending on the
play you are investigating. The character is going to
be interviewed by the audience members, so you
could set the scene on a chatshow, in a police
investigation room or a court, for example,
depending on the context. For instance, if you are
investigating Arthur Miller's *Death of a Salesman*,
you might choose a current affairs television
programme and could begin:

> *Ladies and gentlemen, welcome to the Bronx,
> where tonight we're going undercover to find out
> what life is really like for the locals. Here we have
> Willy Loman, a salesman. Who'd like to ask him
> the first question?*

Then pick audience members to ask the character
questions. The actor in the hotseat must use both
his knowledge of the play and improvisation skills in
order to answer each question fully. Anything he
does not know from the text, he can make up
spontaneously. After each interview ask the class
which of the answers were rooted in information
we find in the play, and which information we are
not told and the actor must have improvised. You
may like to suggest that the audience can ask
questions as their own characters, if appropriate.

The Aim of the Game

The aims of the game are twofold; firstly, it hones
improvisation skills, and secondly, it encourages

participants to investigate a characterisation in detail and to assess their own knowledge of the text.

Variations and Extensions

In order to expand the game, it is often interesting to introduce more than one character. Perhaps they have been brought on to a television programme to talk about themselves. In this way we can also meet the unseen characters from the play. Perhaps the setting might be a trial, in which case the entire group can become involved as witnesses, judge and jury.

Players	Age	Time	Skills
Any, in pairs	10+	20	Analysis, Imagination, Improvisation

PART EIGHT

STORYTELLING

Wally's Wallet

An imaginative game in which players have to create a 'back story' based on an object.

How to Play

This game takes a little preparation but is very worthwhile and often produces dramatic results. Give the group a 'lost object'; e.g. a wallet, a bag with its contents, an old book with a message inside, a wooden box containing old photographs. The object you choose should hold some kind of clue towards the identity of its owner or perhaps the circumstances of its loss.

This game has two variations. To play the short version, give the group several minutes thinking time, and then pass the object around the circle. Each player must tell us the 'true story' behind the object. They may wish to do this in character as someone involved in the story.

To play the extended version, split everyone into groups of up to five players. Give them a several minutes to invent a short story behind the object, then several minutes to prepare an improvisation of the story, using the object as a prop. You might choose to give each group a different object, but often the most rewarding work comes from seeing the variety of stories that can arise from a single stimulus.

The Aim of the Game

This game provides a focused creative opportunity for storytelling and devising. The short version benefits individuals by giving them confidence in their own powers of invention. The longer version teaches participants to collaborate on the creation of a narrative as a team: a difficult skill to master, but one that can be improved with practice.

+ Assorted 'lost objects'			
Players	**Age**	**Time**	**Skills**
Any number	8+	15	Imagination, Teamwork, Improvisation

Super-sized Stories

A game that requires players to be as melodramatic as possible, through exaggeration and comic addition.

How to Play

Ask the group to split into pairs. Each of the players must then tell their partners a true story from their past. Once the two players have swapped stories, they join up with another pair and swap partners to form two new pairs (e.g. if Peggy and Don were a pair, and Muriel and John were a pair, Peggy should go with Muriel and Don with John).

Now they tell their original partner's story to their new partner, only this time they must increase the drama of the story by fifty per cent. They may choose to exaggerate facts, add description, gestures, sound effects, dialogue and detail, adapting the story for dramatic impact.

Now ask the pairs to join up with another new pair, and swap partners again. Now each player must retell the story from their second partner with a further fifty per cent increase in the drama. After swapping stories again, the players must each perform the third story they heard, complete with fifty per cent of their own personal elaborations, to the rest of the group. They will be amazed to hear how their own stories have changed. A discussion about what made the stories interesting to watch encourages players to analyse the elements of an effective narrative and performance.

The Aim of the Game

This simple game encourages players to explore the notion of 'dramatisation', and to discover how they can become more effective and entertaining storytellers. It is interesting to discuss which was the most engaging level of storytelling. Most often these are the halfway stories, as too much exaggeration tends to distance the audience; a worthwhile lesson to remember in drama.

Players	Age	Time	Skills
8+ *in pairs*	**8+**	**20**	*Imagination, Memory, Confidence*

Story Circle

A team storytelling game in which a group devise a narrative together using everyone's input.

How to Play

This is a very simple, creative game in which groups create stories together in a very short amount of time. There are several versions of this activity.

In the first, a story is built word by word. Ask the group to sit in a circle. One person begins with a single word and the players take turns to add a word until a story is created.

As an alternative, you may wish to use sentences rather than single words, to allow the story to build up quickly. If so, ask each person to end their sentence with 'And then…' in order to cue in the next player.

The Aim of the Game

This is a highly creative teamwork activity. The game provides an ideal starting point for a workshop on storytelling. You might want to use it as a starter activity before an improvisation to create the beginning of a story, which the group can then perform.

Variations and Extensions

A variation of this game is to 'pass the story baton'. Choose an object. Whoever holds this object must tell the story. You can either get the group to sit in a circle and pass the baton between players, or ask them to move around the room, acting out the story and passing the baton between them. Whichever way you decide to play, encourage the group to pass the baton at exciting moments, whenever they reach a cliffhanger. This way everyone stays on their toes, listens carefully and has to think quickly.

As a further extension, you can set a theme or give a prop as a stimulus for the story.

+ 'Baton' or a prop for stimulus			
Players	**Age**	**Time**	**Skills**
Any number	8+	10	*Imagination, Teamwork*

Hilari-tales

An imaginative game in which players have to perform fairy tales with a twist, in a range of different dramatic styles.

How to Play

Ask for a suggestion of a well-known fairy tale. Choose a cast and a narrator from the assembled players; the rest of the group become the audience. The fairy tale is now going to become a 'Hilari-tale', a hilarious, wacky version of the original, performed in a new style.

Ask the cast to stand at the side of the playing space, ready to enter when it reaches their part of the story. The narrator must then begin telling the story, whilst the cast act it out.

You then shout 'Freeze!' at a moment of your choice. Ask for suggestions for a style from the watching audience. The cast and narrator must then continue the fairy tale in this particular style, adapting their voices, movement, characterisation and facial expressions according to the suggestion.

Styles that work particularly well include romance, horror, Shakespeare, silent movie, tragedy, American teen-flick, mime, children's TV, musical theatre, opera, slow motion, *Thunderbirds*, *Indiana Jones*, *James Bond*, ballet, gangster, Arnold Schwarzenegger, rap, etc. Or you can use styles of theatre with an advanced group: Victorian melodrama, naturalism, Greek tragedy, agitprop, Theatre of the Absurd, Restoration comedy, vaudeville, etc.

The Aim of the Game

This game is a creative group game that promotes focused improvisation, spontaneity and teamwork. It is also an excellent starting point for looking at styles of drama and investigating genre.

Players	Age	Time	Skills
Any number	10+	20	Improvisation, Imagination

The Great Guild of Archaeologists

An imaginative game in which players have to invent a purpose for an unidentified object on an archaeological dig.

How to Play

Ask the group to sit in a circle. Welcome them to the annual meeting of the Great Guild of Archaeologists, and introduce yourself as Professor Digalot (or another invented archaeologist of your choice). Announce that today you have exciting news: there has been a fabulous new discovery. A strange object was uncovered at the dig, and no one knows what it is. You would now like each of the assembled archaeologists to give you their expert opinions on what the object is, when it was made, and what it was used for. You are sure that one of them is likely to know; after all, they are the greatest archaeologists in the world!

Then bring out the object. I prefer to use something that the players are unfamiliar with: an antique object, metal implement or unusual-looking wooden tool. However, you can easily use something modern and recognisable in order to test their powers of imagination; a broom, for instance, or a fork. Sometimes these familiar objects create the most amusing responses when given a new purpose.

Now pass the object around the circle, giving each player the opportunity to look at it, exploring its features. While they are passing it round, you can offer some opinions you have collected from 'other experts', in order to get them thinking. If you are using a broom, for example, you might comment:

> *Professor Pook from Norway thinks this is an Ancient Roman object, worn on a helmet as a plume. The long wooden section would stick out several feet above the gladiator's head to make them look important. Professor Chan from Beijing disagrees. She thinks it is a nostril-hair comb, used by the Ancient Chinese giants to clean inside their noses. In my own expert opinion, I think it is a musical instrument from Medieval Britain, which could be played like this...* (Demonstrate using the object.) *What do you think, Professor?*

Each player must then tell us the story behind the object, demonstrating its purpose and using the object as a prop. Encourage them to do this in character, inventing their names and where they are from. After giving their explanation, they pass the object on to the next player.

The Aim of the Game

This game is an imaginative exercise that promotes invention, storytelling and devising. It allows the players to be creative in a focused manner, using the object and context as a stimulus. As such, it can be an excellent starter exercise for longer improvisation activities.

Variations and Extensions

This game can easily be extended towards the creation of short scenes, using the object as a starting point. Split the players into groups and give them several minutes together to invent a story behind the object. They then have to improvise this scene. The other groups must then guess which period the object is from and what its purpose is. You can either choose to give each group a different object, or to ask them to find their own interpretation from the single stimulus.

STORYTELLING

+ Assorted random objects			
Players	**Age**	**Time**	**Skills**
Any number	8+	15	Imagination, Teamwork, Improvisation

Illustration Station

In this game, most suitable for younger groups, the players have to create instant physical illustrations to accompany a story.

How to Play

Choose a story full of colourful description and outlandish characters; e.g. Roald Dahl's *Dirty Beasts* and *Revolting Rhymes*. Explain to the group that they are the workers at the 'Illustration Station', the special place where the pictures in books are painted! They must listen very carefully to the story in order to paint the pictures in glorious detail. Every time you clap, they must jump up and create a tableau to illustrate that moment in the story. The only rule is they are not allowed to talk. When they hear you clap again, they must sit down and listen to the next part, until the next time you clap.

Begin reading the story, and choose suitable points to add 'illustrations'. You can add a further challenge by moving around their tableau and tapping players on the head, at which point they must improvise a suitable line for their characters.

With younger players, you may wish to cast the story before you begin. One of the most interesting challenges, however, is working together as a team and sharing the roles without talking. It should not matter who plays who. Encourage them to include as much detail in the scene as possible. If they do not have a character to play, what object might they be? They can be chairs, tables, doorways, scenery – the possibilities are endless.

The Aim of the Game

The group must work together effectively to create each dynamic picture. After the game, it may be useful to discuss which elements of the task they found difficult, and how they can best work together in a team.

+ Short story			
Players	**Age**	**Time**	**Skills**
Any number	6+	20	Imagination, Listening, Mime

Living Newspapers

A creative game for older players in which they have to create a living version of a newspaper front page.

How to Play

Divide the group into teams of approximately four. Give each group the front page of a newspaper. Ask them to spend three minutes noticing everything they can about the page – what do the articles say, what fonts are used, what do the pictures show, are there adverts, what is the tone, the colour, the image presented to the reader?

Then ask each group to prepare a short 'performance' of their front page. They should take into account the tones of writing when deciding how to characterise the articles – are they short and snappy, serious and intellectual, sensational, smutty, political, opinionated? Ask them to use volume, movement, space and voice creatively to present the most interesting and appropriate dramatisation they can.

The Aim of the Game

The aim of the game is to explore the notion of theatre as a social force in a dynamic and creative way. The group should aim towards an exciting visual performance. Meanwhile, the task investigates drama's potential as an instrument of cultural expression. The game can lead onto wider discussion of theatre's place as a social and political phenomenon. How does theatre relate to life? Can it change people's lives? Or does it mirror life, enabling people to reflect on their own situations.

+ Selection of newspaper front pages			
Players	**Age**	**Time**	**Skills**
Any number	12+	20	*Imagination, Analysis*

PART NINE

IMAGINATION

Super Chair

A simple creative game in which players have to find a new identity for a commonplace object.

How to Play

Ask all the players to sit in a circle. Place an object in the middle of the circle, something from around the room, like a chair perhaps, or a scarf. Each player then takes it in turn to use this object as something that contrasts to its true purpose. A chair, for instance, might become a post box, a hat or a horse. Try and choose an object that is not too intricate or detailed, to give players the greatest scope.

A scarf is my favourite object for this game, because fabric is so malleable. Encourage the players to experiment by envisioning a different weight or texture, and to use the object as an item of costume to create a new character for themselves – a scarf can be made into a headdress, a grass skirt, a tie, a ninja headband, a karate belt, a pair of handcuffs; there are endless possibilities. It could become a deadly snake, a growing plant, a heavy baton, a musical instrument – in fact, anything the player should choose, providing their animation is clear. The skill is in convincing the audience of the detail and authenticity of the object. You can play this either as a mime game or allow the players to use sound and speech, which is often more fun.

The Aim of the Game

The game encourages participants to think creatively and to aspire towards intricacy and detail in their ideas and performances.

+ Assorted random objects			
Players	**Age**	**Time**	**Skills**
Any number	**6+**	**10**	*Mime, Precision*

The Magical Mystery Box

An imagination game in which players have to take imaginary objects from a box and mime them for the others to guess.

How to Play

Ask the players to sit in a circle. You then mime a box: show them the shape, indicate the weight and demonstrate any special features; a catch, for instance, or flaps. You can take suggestions from them as to what features the box may have.

This mimed box becomes a 'magic box', from which the players can produce anything, rather like Mary Poppins' bottomless bag. The 'box' is passed from player to player. Each takes their turn to open the box and take out a mimed object, which they demonstrate to the group. Try and encourage them to be as detailed as possible, demonstrating the function, size and shape. The other players then have to guess the object. When it has been correctly guessed, the box is passed on to the next player.

The Aim of the Game

This game provides a truly imaginative opportunity as players can mime anything they want. They will be rewarded when others guess their mime, gaining confidence and choosing more difficult mime subjects.

Variations and Extensions

For an interesting adaptation, try using a theme. This can be useful with younger players to stimulate ideas; e.g. Animals or Christmas presents. With older players, themes can make the task more challenging. You may use the game in conjunction with a research task, especially if you are working towards a play set in a particular period or community. The group can come prepared with ideas about what objects they might show from a Victorian schoolroom, the Restoration period or Ancient Greece, for instance.

Players	Age	Time	Skills
Any number	6+	10	*Mime, Precision*

137

No, Not Me!

An imaginative guessing game in which players have to justify their character's worth in order to be saved.

How to Play

In this game, you play Old Mr (or Mrs) Norman, who is finally cleaning out the house after many years of collecting junk. You need to decide what to throw away, and you are determined to get rid of lots of the old rubbish.

Ask the players to get into groups of approximately four. In their groups they need to choose a room in the house. Then, within their groups, they must each choose an object in that room, which they will represent. Next, they must all think of a reason why their object is invaluable to Old Mr/s Norman. They should be able to articulate the reason without saying the name of their object. For instance, 'You can't throw me away because otherwise you would have to sleep on the floor, and that would hurt!' (a bed) or 'You can't throw me away or all your food would get warm and go mouldy!' (a fridge). When they have chosen their self-defensive justifications, ask the first group to come into the space and take their positions as their objects. The other groups watch carefully.

You then mime opening the door to the room, looking around in disgust, and deciding that most of the rubbish needs throwing away. Approach the first player. You say 'I think I will throw *you* away.' They must reply 'No, not me!', to which you say 'Not you? Why not?!' Then they must give their answer: 'You can't throw me away because…'

The watching players then guess what that object is. Once they have guessed correctly, move on to the next object in the room and repeat the process. After all four of the objects have been guessed, ask the watching players to guess which room in the house the objects were in.

The Aim of the Game

The game promotes verbal skills, as each player justifies their object's importance, and mime skills in their portrayal of the objects. It also encourages the players to work as a team.

Variations and Extensions

There are numerous versions of this game. *Not Me, Noah!* is an interesting alternative, in which Noah decides which animals to take on to the Ark. Each of the players must choose an animal to mime and justify their reason for being allowed on board. Instead of guessing the room, players have to guess the animal family (mammals, reptiles, birds).

You can also set this game at the *Gates of Heaven*, with famous people having to bid for their place inside!

Players	Age	Time	Skills
8+	6+	15	*Mime, Vocabulary*

Bomb and Shield

An energetic, creative game that often leads on to extended improvisations. It involves players moving around quickly before creating scenarios from their scattered positions.

How to Play

Ask the players to spread out around the room. Tell them to choose another player to be their personal 'bomb'. They must give no indication of who they have chosen. Then ask them to choose another player to be their 'shield', again giving no indication as to whom they have selected. When you say 'Go!', the group need to move around the room, attempting to keep their 'shield' between themselves and the 'bomb' at all times.

On your instruction, they should all begin to move, and patterns will form instantly as each individual tries to keep in line with the shield and bomb they have chosen. After a short time, shout 'Freeze!' At this point they must all stop immediately and remain in their exact position. Ask them, without moving significantly, to look around the room at the frozen picture they have created. Ask them to raise their hands if they can see a scene within this picture. Choose one of these individuals to initiate the scene they imagined, at which point the rest of the players must unfreeze and join in. For instance, Jim is chosen to begin a scene – he notices that most players are frozen in a running position, so he says 'On your marks, get set, go!' The other players, on hearing this, respond to Jim's initiating line and begin acting as if they are in a race.

The Aim of the Game

This game aims to encourage both creativity and focus. It also demands spontaneity in the immediate reactions that are necessary in the second part of the game. It is a game that groups often become more skilled at with time, as they become more ambitious and adventurous with the scene ideas they suggest.

Players	Age	Time	Skills
10+	10+	15	*Imagination, Improvisation, Focus*

Word Wizard

An imaginative mime game in which players have to guess the word you are thinking of by acting out various possibilities.

How to Play

Ask the players to sit in a circle. You are the 'Word Wizard', and begin the game by saying 'I am thinking of a word that rhymes with… cat' or an alternative word of your choice. The players then take it in turns to come into the middle of the circle and mime their guesses. One might mime using a cricket bat, one wearing a hat, one wiping his feet on a mat. The rest of the group has to guess what they are miming. When the group has guessed the word, you can tell the actor if it was the one you were thinking of. If they were right, then they become the Word Wizard.

This game is very appealing to older players, especially when you use words that have many obscure rhymes. Words that work well include 'shoe' (brew, two, new, knew, loo, crew, do, few, boo, goo, hue, Jew, sue, etc.), 'bear' (share, care, lair, fair, dare, hair, mare, tear, rare, pair, pear, etc.) and 'boot' (toot, flute, newt, mute, coot, moot, loot, fruit, suit, root, etc.). This challenges the players to mime abstract nouns and verbs, which are often much more interesting than the simple nouns that younger players suggest.

The Aim of the Game

The game promotes mime skills and imagination, but also encourages players to widen their vocabulary.

Players	Age	Time	Skills
Any number	**6+**	**10**	*Mime, Vocabulary, Focus*

Why Don't We...

A simple improvisation game that encourages positivity and teaches players not to 'block'.

How to Play

Ask the players to find a partner, let's use Lindsey and Kristin as our players.

There are three rounds in this game: the negative, the neutral and the positive.

In the first round, the 'negative round', Lindsey offers Kristin suggestions of activities they could do together, 'Why don't we...?' Each time Kristin must block the idea and make an excuse: 'No, because...' For example:

> LINDSEY: Why don't we go to the cinema?
>
> KRISTIN: No, because I'm allergic to popcorn.
>
> LINDSEY: Why don't we go and play on the beach?
>
> KRISTIN: No, because it's freezing today and I don't have a coat to wear.
>
> LINDSEY: Why don't we go skydiving?
>
> KRISTIN: No, because I am scared of flying... and heights.

Encourage them to make their suggestions and responses as original as possible, avoiding 'No, because I don't want to' and 'No, because I don't like...' After a few minutes, swap over. Then move on to the second, 'neutral' round.

This time, when Kristin offers a suggestion, Lindsey responds with an excuse and an alternative.

> KRISTIN: Why don't we go scuba-diving?
>
> LINDSEY: No, scuba-diving's too scary, but we could go swimming.
>
> KRISTIN: Why don't we go to an art class?
>
> LINDSEY: No, I can't draw, but we could go to an art gallery and buy a painting.
>
> KRISTIN: Why don't we fly to Mars?
>
> LINDSEY: No, because we don't have a spaceship, but we could fly to Paris.

Once both players have had a turn, move on to the final, 'positive' round, in which each player accepts and builds on each other's suggestions.

> LINDSEY: Why don't we watch *Dr Who*?
>
> KRISTIN: Yes! And then we could build our own time machine!
>
> LINDSEY: Yes! And then we could go back to Medieval times!
>
> KRISTIN: Yes! And then we could dance at a castle ball!
>
> LINDSEY: Yes! And then we could meet a handsome prince!
>
> KRISTIN: Yes! And then I could marry him!
>
> LINDSEY: Yes! And then I could marry his gorgeous brother!

Allow this third round to continue until the pairs find a natural conclusion for their 'And then…' stories. You might like to watch the pairs perform their stories to the rest of the group.

Ask the players to observe how the energy in each round changed according to the nature of the responses. The first round inevitably has low energy because every idea is blocked (stopped). As a consequence, the scene cannot progress. The neutral round has a little more energy, but it is only when actors accept and develop each other's improvisation suggestions that a narrative can develop and the scene finally becomes exciting and energetic. This is an important principle in any improvisation work.

The Aim of the Game

The game encourages supportiveness and acceptance in improvisation scenarios, so that ideas and inventiveness do not get blocked.

Players	Age	Time	Skills
Any, in pairs	8+	20	Improvisation, Awareness

Alien Interview

An amusing improvisation game in which an interpreter has to translate an alien's gibberish responses.

How to Play

Ask the players to get into groups of three, and to name themselves A, B and C.

Explain to them that Earth has recently been visited by aliens (As), and that we are lucky enough to have some of them with us today. Unfortunately, they only speak 'Alienese', so they have trained some humans to be their translators (Bs). Today the panel of scientists (Cs) will be interviewing the aliens, in order to find out as much as possible about life on their planet.

Then ask each trio to find a space and begin the improvisation. The scientist in each group then begins to ask the alien interesting questions, via the translator. Encourage the scientist to think of inventive and appropriate questions; e.g.

'How did you get here?'
'What do the aliens on your planet look like?'
'What is the weather like there?'
'What do you eat?'
'What do you do for fun?'
'How do you catch you food?'
'What are aliens scared of?'
'What do you think of humans?'

The translator puts these question into Alienese (gibberish), using gestures and appropriate tones. The alien then answers in Alienese, using movements, facial expressions, sounds and gibberish to convey their answers back to the translator, who must interpret them for the interviewer. The interpreter must take the alien's tones and expressions into account when translating their message.

This game often results in very inventive scenes and hilarious answers, so make sure you allow time for the groups to watch each other, picking the best questions that they asked to show to the rest of the group.

The Aim of the Game

This game helps build a wealth of skills for players. It encourages players to create inventive answers using their physical, vocal and improvisational skills. It also demands careful observation skills on the part of the translator, who must spontaneously interpret the alien's answers based on their vocal and physical expressions. For the scene to be successful, the trio has to work closely together, maintaining awareness of the development of the scene, and creating new questions and answers appropriately.

IMAGINATION

Players	Age	Time	Skills
Any, in threes	8+	15	Mime, Spontaneity, Improvisation

IMAGINATION

Pantomime Race

A fast-paced improvisation game that involves the whole group in creating spontaneous scenarios.

How to Play

Ask the group to form a line along one side of the playing space. The first player, let's call him Charlie, runs into the space and begins to perform an imaginary activity of his choice. It could be anything. Charlie chooses racing a car. The next player in the line, Chris, then runs into the space and says 'What are you doing?' Charlie can answer anything except 'Racing a car.' He says 'Can't you see? I'm chasing a pig!' The moment Chris hears this, he must begin miming Charlie's stated activity. Off he goes, chasing an imaginary pig around the room, complete with an array of appropriate sound effects. Meanwhile, Charlie runs off and joins the back of the line. Then Stu, the next person in line, runs in and says 'What are you doing?' and the game continues, with each new player miming the activity that the current player says they are doing – though actually aren't.

Before long, players realise the potential comedy to be had from giving the next player an outlandish activity: 'Can't you see? I am doing brain surgery with a banana!' or 'Can't you see? I am trying to swim through melting marshmallows whilst singing musical theatre!' Encourage the group to be as inventive as possible.

The Aim of the Game

The aim is to get players' imaginations flowing, to build energy and to help them realise that there is no 'wrong' answer in creative activities. The fact that anything goes in this game makes it a great icebreaker, and helps to build rapport between the players.

Players	Age	Time	Skills
4+	**8+**	**10**	*Focus, Mime*

PART TEN

IMPROVISATION

Speed Scene

A fast-paced team game in which everyone contributes to a super-speedy spontaneous scenario.

How to Play

Ask the players to line up along one side of the playing area. When you shout 'Go!' the players must run into the space and add themselves into a frozen scene. Usually gameplay goes something like this:

KIM: (*The first in line, running into the space and taking a position.*) I am a friendly policewoman on the beat.

DEANA: (*The next in line, following suit.*) I am a thief sneaking away.

PENNY: (*Running in and freezing.*) I am the grandma whose bag the thief stole.

MOIRA: (*Running in and freezing.*) I am a local punk who tries to stop the thief.

The game continues until everyone is on stage in a frozen position. You may wish to stop the scene here and play again. Alternatively, if you wish to explore dialogue and voice, you can tap each character on the shoulder, and they must improvise a line of dialogue in character.

You can simply ask the players to bring the scene to life, and to improvise what happens next. Or you could ask them to bring it to life in slow motion, or as a mime. The group could also repeat the exercise, creating tableaux of what happened one minute before the scene, and one minute afterwards, building a story in three pictures. You can then ask them to improvise the whole story, from tableau one, through two, to three. This could provide a starting point for discussing the importance of a definite beginning, middle and end in a narrative.

The Aim of the Game

The aim is to create an exciting, dynamic and cohesive scene as a team.

Players	Age	Time	Skills
Any number	8+	15	Confidence, Spontaneity, Character

Freeze!

Many actors' favourite improvisation game, in which players jump in and out of scenes, creating new scenarios whenever they see an opportunity.

How to Play

Choose two volunteers to start an improvisation. It can be anything, from two grannies at a market to a pair of garden gnomes talking about the view. They should be encouraged to begin spontaneously, with the first idea that comes to mind.

The other players watch, waiting for an opportunity to 'freeze' the improvisation and swap with one of the actors. They must wait until they see a player take a position that they could fit into a new scenario; a pirate looking through his telescope may become a man eating a baguette, for example. When a player sees such an opportunity, they shout 'Freeze!' The two actors freeze immediately where they are, and the new player walks in and replaces one of them, taking the exact physical position. The new actor then begins a new improvisation, which the other actor must respond to immediately. This scene continues until someone else shouts 'Freeze!'

The players should be encouraged to change the scenarios entirely when they begin a new scene. Otherwise, players are tempted to simply adapt an argument scene into another row with slightly different characters. Players may transform into animals, objects, famous people, whatever catches their imaginations.

The Aim of the Game

The game promotes strong improvisation skills, and improves players' ability to act spontaneously. It is also a good method of teaching the group not to block each other's ideas. Players will soon learn that if one actor begins 'What have you done with my T-shirt?' and the other replies 'What are you talking about… I'm a lizard!', the improvisation will soon grind to a halt!

Players	Age	Time	Skills
Any number	8+	15	Spontaneity, Teamwork, Character

Cocktail Party

A hilarious, structured improvisation game in which the 'host' has to identify each of the weird and wonderful guests at the party.

How to Play

Choose about six volunteers from the group. The remaining participants become the audience. The first volunteer is the 'party host', and waits outside the room whilst the other volunteers, the 'guests', are allocated characters.

It is best to pick a range of character types, some famous people, types of animals, professions (see the list below for suggestions). With older groups, you might want to allocate some guests specific character traits, strange obsessions, habits or phobias; a love of toe hair, for instance, a fear of fizzy drinks, or a great urge to wash every few minutes. These characters are harder to guess but provide a greater challenge for the actors, and more amusement for the audience!

Once the characters have been selected, invite the host back in to the room. The host improvises setting up the party, putting chairs out, pouring imaginary drinks, until you make a doorbell sound effect, to indicate that a guest has arrived. At this point, the host mimes opening the door, and welcomes the guest in. The host has to try and guess who or what the guest is, and may ask them questions in order to do so. The guest must remain physically in character throughout. Add each of the guests until all are present. The host must continue to guess whilst hosting the party. Each time he guesses correctly, that character leaves the party and sits back down with the audience.

The challenge in this game is for the actors to reveal their characters subtly, without allowing the host to guess too quickly! Try and encourage the host to involve the guests in party-related activities and conversations, to give the actors the best opportunities to reveal their characteristics. The host could offer some food or drinks, ask what they've been doing today, or whether they fancy a dance. Actors should be encouraged to experiment with ways to suggest their characters, through gestures, conversation and suggestive answers; e.g. 'Ham sandwiches? Yuck, no thanks, have you got any cheese?' (A mouse.)

*

Other character suggestions include:

Animals: Try and choose animals that have recognisable characteristics, food habits and movements that everyone will be familiar with. A mouse is much easier to portray than a duck-billed platypus! Most farmyard animals are suitable; other interesting animals include giraffes, fish, kangaroos, snakes, rats, rabbits, camels, lions and lizards.

Famous People: Choose characters who everyone in the audience will definitely recognise; e.g. the Queen, the Prime Minister, celebrities like Elvis or Madonna. You can pick sports personalities or television celebrities, or, if you are playing in a school or youth group, you may want to pick teachers or group leaders (as long as they are not easily offended!).

Occupations: Interesting professions to choose include actors, firemen, doctors, therapists, cleaners, mad scientists, teachers, explorers, soldiers and chefs.

Character Traits: It's easiest to choose ideas that relate to a party situation, to give the actors a helping hand; someone obsessed with balloons, for example, someone with a pizza phobia or who is scared of party hats. Otherwise, physical fixations are amusing – obsessions with belly buttons, ears or hair colour; or compulsive habits – like cleaning, shouting, dancing, sleeping or eating.

The Aim of the Game

The host must use their observation and questioning skills to guess the identities of their guests as quickly as possible, whilst the guests experiment with characterisation in a creative and amusing way.

Players	Age	Time	Skills
8+	**12+**	**15**	*Character, Spontaneity, Imagination*

One-Minute Wonder

A very simple yet creative game, in which actors have to speak for one minute on a random subject.

How to Play

Simply choose a player and give them a topic. For older players, the more random the topic, the better; 'Custard', 'Nose Clippings' or 'Jellied Eels', for instance. For younger players you might choose to give them the option of talking about a favourite hobby or school subject, something they are confident speaking about.

The player must then stand up and speak for one minute (or however long you feel appropriate) on their topic. The rules are that they must not hesitate (pause for over three seconds), deviate from the subject significantly, or repeat key words, facts or phrases. They should also be discouraged from adding hesitant 'ums' and 'ers'. If another player feels that the speaker has broken one of these rules he must call out 'Stop!' and state his case. If you agree with his accusation, then he takes over from the speaker. The winner is whoever is speaking when one minute is up.

The Aim of the Game

This game not only encourages quick thinking and inventiveness, but eloquence and confidence. Speaking in front of a group can be very intimidating, but in this game the speaker's mind is occupied by the topic and the clock, so they tend to forget to be nervous.

Players	Age	Time	Skills
Any number	10+	10	Vocabulary, Focus, Spontaneity

Gossip Stream

An improvisation game in which players invent a stream of gossip as a team.

How to Play

Ask the players to stand in a circle. Tiptoe across the circle to a player of your choice, let's call her Lynn, and stage-whisper a juicy piece of gossip to her; e.g. 'Did you know… that Jamie found something shocking under his bed this morning?!' The whole group then responds with a melodramatic, shocked intake of breath, 'Uhhh!'

Lynn then completes the piece of gossip, 'Yes, and… I heard it was a mouldy piece of brie – that Jess put there!' The rest of the group then responds 'No!!' in an equally melodramatic fashion. You then take Lynn's place in the circle.

It is then Lynn's turn to tiptoe across the circle to another player, Ray. She then repeats the story so far: 'Did you know that Jess put a mouldy piece of brie under Jamie's bed?' The group responds with their intake of breath – 'Uhhh!' – then Ray completes the line of gossip, adding 'Yes, and… I heard it was a trap for the mysterious cheese thief!' The group responds 'No!!' Lynn takes Ray's place, and Ray goes to another player to continue the gossip stream.

Carry on, encouraging the players to make the story increasingly dramatic, and their reactions more and more exaggerated, until the story reaches its conclusion with the final member of the circle.

The Aim of the Game

This game encourages its players to explore melodrama and exaggeration, whilst contributing creatively to a story as a group.

Players	Age	Time	Skills
Any number	**8+**	**10**	*Imagination, Listening, Dynamism*

Bus-stop Banter

A quick-fire improvisation game that requires actors to sustain a conversation whilst rapidly changing characters.

How to Play

Choose two players to be 'up', let's call them Alex and Sian. Give them a conversation topic. It could be as simple as 'the weather' or as obscure as 'Which would you rather be, a badger or a snake?' Ensure that you choose topics which will sustain the two players in conversation for several minutes.

They must begin the improvisation as if they were two strangers conversing at a bus stop. When they have got going, shout in a circumstance. They must continue their conversation, without breaking the flow or forgetting they are waiting for the bus, but now incorporating the new circumstance. A circumstance could be any of the following:

A new identity
   'You are both old ladies.'
   'Alex is a pupil and Sian is the teacher.'
   'You are both firefighters.'
   'You are husband and wife.'

A new situation
   'You are both underwater.'
   'You are boiling hot.'
   'You both have the plague.'
   'You realise you are standing in quicksand.'

A new objective
   'Alex wants Sian's watch.'
   'Sian wants to hypnotise Alex.'
   'Alex wants to seduce Sian.'
   'You both want to be first on the bus.'

See how well they can sustain the scene. Choose two new players, give them a fresh conversation topic, and begin again.

The Aim of the Game

The aim of the game is for the actors to be as inventive as possible whilst sustaining the scene, so it is an excellent exercise in maintaining focus and being spontaneous. There are endless inventive possibilities and hours of hilarity to be had with this exercise. With older players, you can make the game much more difficult by choosing obscure conversational topics; questions they can debate often work particularly well. Encourage them to relate the content of what they are saying to the circumstance they are playing; e.g. how might Sian use the content of the conversation to try and seduce Alex?

Players	Age	Time	Skills
Any number	8+	15	Imagination, Spontaneity, Character

Dramategories

An imaginative team game in which players have to invent a scene incorporating a randomly chosen person, place and object.

How to Play

Split the group into numbered teams of between four and six players. Explain that you are going to give three 'dramategories' (categories) with which they are going to build a scene.

The first dramategory is famous people. Each team must choose one person that everyone in the group has heard of; e.g. Harry Potter, the Queen, Marilyn Monroe.

Ask each group to name their chosen person, and then allocate each suggestion to the next group number up (e.g. with four groups, group 1 gives to group 2, 2 to 3, 3 to 4, and 4 to 1).

Next, each group must think of an interesting place. It could be somewhere specific (on top of the Empire State Building); it could be a building (in a bakery) or somewhere vaguer (like on the moon or in Africa). Ask each group to name their place, and then allocate each suggestion to the group number one lower than theirs (e.g. group 4 gives to 3, 3 to 2, etc.).

Finally, ask each group to think of an unusual object; anything from a lemon squeezer to a magic wand, a vacuum cleaner to a grass skirt. This time they are allocated their own object.

Each group then has ten minutes to create a scene involving the character, in the chosen place, with the chosen object. Their scene must involve all the players and incorporate a definite beginning, middle and end. Emphasise that each element must be instrumentally involved in the plot; e.g. if given Indiana Jones, a school playground and a guitar, they cannot just create a playground scene in which, at some point, for no apparent reason, Indiana Jones walks through, guitar in hand!

*

Why the complicated numbers?
After many times playing this game, divvying out

suggestions in various ways, I began to notice how commonly teams pick easy suggestions for themselves and purposely suggest near impossible ideas for other groups. This version is a fail-safe way of ensuring that, if they try this, it'll bite them back! By allocating the first two suggestions to other groups and the third to themselves, you ensure that, if they pick a difficult third suggestion on purpose, assuming it will be given away, they are stuck with it! The next time you play the game, vary the way of distributing the ideas to ensure they never know who will be given their ideas.

The Aim of the Game

The aim of this game is to encourage players to creative inventive, original stories using ideas that they would never have chosen to put together, therefore encouraging them to think more widely about the possibilities of narrative in drama. It also demands teamwork and concentration, as the groups have to create a scene under time constraints.

Variations and Extensions

You can very easily vary the dramategories in this game. Other good categories include a time period (prehistoric, 1960s, futuristic), a style (horror, romance, *Thunderbirds*) or a line of dialogue.

You can also give each group an item of costume or a prop for added hilarity and inventiveness.

Players	Age	Time	Skills
12+	8+	25	*Imagination, Teamwork*

Death by Chocolate

An improvisation game in which players have to adapt their scenes to feature a random death... during performance!

How to Play

Split the groups into teams of four or more. Give each team the title of a scene which they now have five minutes to prepare. Their scene must not be longer than one minute, and it must have a beginning, middle and end. It is useful to carry a list of inventive scene titles with you, some suggestions might include:

The Shock under the Bed
The Queen's Secret
Harry Potter and the Goblet of Ribena
Nightclub Nightmare
Gone with the Window Man
What's in the Well?
The Other Side of the Door
Journey into Space
The Magic Toy
The Secret of the Seventh Sea
The Stolen Booty

When five minutes are up, choose a team to go first. Explain that, at some point during their performance, you are going to shout out 'Death by...' followed by a random word; e.g. toothpaste, cotton wool, orange juice, banana split, sofa, bedpost, jelly, guitar, etc. – the less dangerous the object, the harder the challenge and the more amusing the performance! If you prefer, rather than shouting out, you can put the object words on cards and allow an audience member to pick one without looking. This adds a little more mystery and tension.

Their task is to incorporate a death by that object within the scene, before their one minute is up. They must incorporate it naturally as part of the action; someone cannot suddenly keel over dead with no explanation. The scene must then reach a conclusion by the time you reach the end of the minute.

Do not tell the group that you are playing 'Death by…' at the beginning of the game. Wait until they have created and rehearsed their scenes, or they will plan a death into their stories!

The Aim of the Game

The aim is to help the players learn to react spontaneously to whatever is thrown at them during a scene. They cannot plan the death, as they don't know it is coming, or at least what it will be, so they have no choice but to improvise it during their performance. This helps them learn to think on their feet, and to cope with unplanned events during performance.

+ List of scenes and 'Death by…' categories			
Players	**Age**	**Time**	**Skills**
4+	10+	20	*Imagination, Teamwork, Spontaneity*

Rub-a-dub-dub

An improvisation game in which players have to provide the dubbing for a silent scene.

How to Play

Choose four players to be 'up'. Two will be silent actors and two will provide the voice-overs.

Now give the two silent actors a scene title, without letting the voice-over actors see (giving them a title on a piece of paper works well). Simple titles work best; e.g. *Jungle Expedition*, *The Surprise Present* or *The Stolen Wallet*. The silent actors then must begin improvising the scene, in the most expressive and animated way they can, whilst staying totally silent.

The voice-over actors must stand on opposite sides of the stage. Their challenge is to improvise the sound for the scene, which can include voice-overs for the characters, and any appropriate sound effects.

At the natural conclusion of the scene (or after a few minutes, if the scene shows no sign of stopping), freeze the scene and ask the actors dubbing it to guess the title of the scene. Whilst the guesses are sometimes surprisingly accurate, often they will be strikingly different from the original scene title!

The Aim of the Game

Players must create the most interesting scene possible, both vocally and physically, whilst working with the constriction that only half of them know what the scene is! It is a good exercise, therefore, in collaboration and teamwork.

+ List of scenes			
Players	**Age**	**Time**	**Skills**
4+	**10+**	**10**	*Imagination, Teamwork, Spontaneity*

Sit, Stand, Lie Down

A fast-paced improvisation game in which players have to maintain a scene whilst changing physical positions on stage.

How to Play

Set a chair in the centre of the playing space. Ask for three volunteers and give them a scenario. Something relatively simple often works most effectively; e.g. 'The doctor's surgery', 'Bully in the playground', 'Lost in the woods' or 'A day at the zoo'.

The rule of the improvisation is that there must always be one player sitting on the chair, one standing, and one lying on the ground. When one moves to another position, the other two must swap around to compensate, justifying their change of position within the scene.

For instance, in a doctor's surgery, let's imagine that our three characters are the doctor, the nurse and the patient. The patient logically begins lying on the bed, the doctor standing up, choosing a medical instrument, and the nurse perhaps sitting, taking the patient's temperature. If the actor playing the patient stands up suddenly, maybe scared of the doctor's choice of giant syringe, then the other two must move immediately. Maybe the nurse faints (to lie on the floor) and the doctor sits down in the chair in surprise. The more frequently they move, the more fun the game becomes!

The Aim of the Game

The aim of the game is for the three actors to maintain an entertaining scene, whilst improvising new elements in order to fulfil the rules of the game. The actors quickly become more adept at this and begin to challenge each other by moving more frequently. This is a great game to play with teenage or adult groups.

Players	Age	Time	Skills
Any, in threes	10+	15	Imagination, Teamwork, Spontaneity

Instant Opera

An entertaining game in which players have to sing their text.

How to Play

This is a game aimed at exploring a piece of text within a rehearsal process, although it can easily be played with a random extract from a play or a novel. If you are using a novel extract, then organise who will say each line in advance. A simple way to do so is to get the group into a circle and allocate a sentence each, around the ring.

The aim is to produce a mini improvised operetta or musical version of the script. This is a hilarious activity, but really helps participants to pay attention to the structure and style of the writing.

Each of the actors must sing their part in the most melodramatic way. The challenge is to use the shape and sounds of the words to help you pick an appropriate style of singing. Ask them to look at the way the words appear on the page: is it verse or prose? How long are the sentences? How clipped is the vocabulary? What are the key differences between the characters in the manner that they speak? How is punctuation used? How important are pauses? Where are the dramatic climaxes? Is there any rhyme or repetition, assonance, alliteration or other interesting figures of speech?

When the players have had some preparation time to look at their scripts, begin the game by announcing 'Ladies and gentlemen, welcome to *Hedda Gabler: The Musical*!', or whichever text you have chosen. You may like to sing the stage directions to help get the scene going. Characters must then come on and sing their parts. If you have already blocked the scene (i.e. decided where, when and how actors will move), encourage them to use the blocking as they know it, but exaggerate everything to achieve the melodrama of the musical!

You can encourage the watching players to applaud spectacularly dramatic moments in order to support each other.

The Aim of the Game

This is a dramatic and dynamic way to explore the structure and diction of a written text. It works particularly well for Greek tragedy or Shakespeare, in which you can encourage players to use the rhythms of the verse to give them their song structures.

Variations and Extensions

Pyramus and Thisbe (the play that the mechanicals perform in *A Midsummer Night's Dream*) is an ideal text to use with this game. The contrasts in the tones, structure and language between characters makes for a colourful performance, and there is plenty to discuss afterwards in terms of Shakespeare's purposeful overuse of rhyme, rhythm and metaphor in Bottom's 'odes'.

IMPROVISATION

+ Scripts or text for each player			
Players	**Age**	**Time**	**Skills**
Any number	12+	25	Imagination, Voice, Analysis

PART ELEVEN

COOL-DOWN

Pressure Gauge

A simple relaxation exercise for the end of a session.

How to Play

Ask the players to find a space to lie down on the floor with their eyes closed. Explain that they will need to focus on their bodies in detail, paying attention to every single muscle, in order to relax after all their hard work. It is vital that everyone concentrates fully for the exercise to be beneficial. You might like to explain that their bodies are their instruments, so it is important to be able to focus clearly on what the body is doing.

Begin by asking them to think about their face. Feature by feature, they are going to focus on and tense up each part for three counts, before finally letting go. The trick is to keep the rest of the body relaxed, so that only the part in question is being tensed. You will need to talk the group through this exercise to ensure they remain totally focused:

> *Let's start with the eyes. Now as I count to 3, I want you to screw your eyes up as tight as you can, tensing all those muscles, tight, tight, tight! Ready?*
>
> *1 – tighten those muscles.*
>
> *2 – even tighter, tense every little muscle as much as you can.*
>
> *3 – As tight as they can go!*
>
> *And release – let them all go; feel all your muscles relax. Make sure they are absolutely loose and relaxed. Now let's move down to the nose.*

Once you have moved through the face and neck, work down the body in as much detail as you have time for, including shoulders, chest, upper arms, lower arms, hands, fingers, thumbs, tummy muscles, bottom (this may be too much of a source of amusement for some groups), thighs, calves, ankles and toes. Each time, ask them to consider the specific body part, tense it up as much as possible over three counts, and then 'release', totally relaxing it.

Finally, once you have moved through the whole of the body, part by part, ask each participant to tense their entire bodies, every muscle, for three counts, before releasing. At the end of this exercise they should be totally relaxed.

The Aim of the Game

This game asks players to focus on and observe the feelings in each specific part of their body. Physically, the action of tensing and releasing provides relaxation, whilst encouraging the players to work calmly and maturely towards a specific goal.

Players	Age	Time	Skills
Any number	8+	10	Focus, Relaxation

COOL-DOWN

20 to 1

An 'end of the session' activity in which the group has to calmly work together to count down from 20 to 1 with no overlapping voices.

How to Play

Ask the players to sit in a circle. Explain that you are going to count down from 20 to 1 as a group. Each number must only be said by one person. If anyone speaks at the same time as anyone else, everyone must start again from 20.

You begin. Every time two people say a number at the same time, you should say 20 again to reset the game back to the beginning.

The Aim of the Game

The aim is for the group to work together calmly to get to 1. For this to work, everyone must concentrate and work together as a team, having the patience to try again every time two people speak. Whilst it sometimes takes several attempts, the feeling of success when the group manage to reach their target together is well worth the effort.

Variations and Extensions

If you have less than twenty players, some people will speak more than once. You should discourage any one individual from saying too many numbers to ensure that everyone gets the chance to participate.

If you have more than twenty players you can start a higher number (the same number as there are players) and work down to 1, to ensure everyone has the opportunity to participate.

Players	Age	Time	Skills
10+	10+	10	*Focus, Teamwork, Relaxation*

Ring of Trust

A two-minute activity to create a positive group bond at the end of a session.

How to Play

Ask the players to stand in a circle, all facing clockwise, so they are inches away from the person in front of them. It is imperative that everyone stands very close together.

Explain that, on your count, everyone is going to lower themselves into a sitting position *very slowly*! As you bend your knees, the person in front of you will sit on your knees, and you will sit on the knees of the person behind you. In this way, the group will create a ring of people all sitting comfortably and supported on each other's laps!

Ensure that everyone is standing close enough together, and then count to 3. This may take several attempts, so make sure it is undertaken slowly and carefully, but it is well worth it!

The Aim of the Game

This game is a means of achieving a physical goal together as a group. For it to work, every single player needs to participate and support one another. It is therefore an ideal final game of any session, as it leaves people with a positive feeling of achievement and group solidarity.

Players	Age	Time	Skills
Any number	**10+**	**5**	*Focus, Teamwork, Trust*

CROSS-REFERENCE
INDEX OF GAMES

SKILLS

Analysis
56. Doctor, Doctor!
72. Character Hotseat

Awareness
9. Cat and Mouse
27. Splat!
45. The Imaginatively Titled Yes-No Game
46. Colombian Hypnosis
47. Liar, Liar!
48. Wink Murder
50. Wolf and Sheep
57. Friendly Follower
66. Psychiatrist
68. Pauper to Prince
85. Why Don't We…

Character
10. Pass the Face
12. Funny Face
18. Good Evening, Your Majesty
24. Elbow to Elbow
36. Character Corners
60. Family Portraits
61. Lead With Your…
62. Themed Musical Chairs
63. Grandma's Hat
64. The Ministry of Funny Walks
65. Emotion Machines
66. Psychiatrist
67. Object Puppetry Challenge
68. Pauper to Prince
69. Aces High!
70. Slingshot
71. Max's Motivations
72. Character Hotseat
88. Speed Scene
89. Freeze!
90. Cocktail Party
93. Bus-stop Banter

Confidence
4. Super Shake
7. The Incredible Itch
8. Daily-Routine Disco
10. Pass the Face
11. Ooey, Gooey, Chewy Gum

19. Sing-along Word Association
23. The Amazing 'A's Game
70. Slingshot
74. Super-sized Stories
88. Speed Scene

Coordination
2. Greyhound Race
5. Mirror, Mirror…
35. King of the Jungle
39. Cyclops
43. Relay Rhythms
54. Star Wars

Dynamism
6. Yes, Let's!
28. Whoosh!
29. Yeehah!
40. Zip, Zap, Zoom!
47. Liar, Liar!
92. Gossip Stream

Energy
1. Rubber Chicken!
2. Greyhound Race
5. Mirror, Mirror…
6. Yes, Let's!
20. Anyone Who…
21. Red Ball, Yellow Ball
22. Name Tag
24. Elbow to Elbow
26. Energy Ball
27. Splat!
28. Whoosh!
29. Yeehah!
30. Duck, Duck, Goose!
31. Fruit Salad
32. Shark Attack!
33. Captain Cod
34. Penguin Race
35. King of the Jungle
36. Character Corners
37. Mexican Clap
40. Zip, Zap, Zoom!
41. The Land of Back-to-Front
52. 1, 2, 3, Washing Machine!
55. Enigma
64. The Ministry of Funny Walks

PRACTICALITIES

Advanced Players
6. Yes, Let's!
17. Human Orchestra
19. Sing-along Word Association
21. Red Ball, Yellow Ball
25. I Love You, Honey!
35. King of the Jungle
46. Colombian Hypnosis
47. Liar, Liar!
51. Tableaux
55. Enigma
58. Leap of Faith
66. Psychiatrist
67. Object Puppetry Challenge
68. Pauper to Prince
71. Max's Motivations
72. Character Hotseat
73. Wally's Wallet
74. Super-sized Stories
76. Hilari-tales
77. The Great Guild of Archaeologists
79. Living Newspapers
84. Word Wizard
86. Alien Interview
87. Pantomime Race
89. Freeze!
90. Cocktail Party
91. One-Minute Wonder
93. Bus-stop Banter
94. Dramategories
95. Death by Chocolate
96. Rub-a-dub-dub
97. Sit, Stand, Lie Down
98. Instant Opera

Larger Groups (20+)
1. Rubber Chicken!
2. Greyhound Race
3. MTV Cameraman
4. Super Shake
6. Yes, Let's!
8. Daily-Routine Disco
9. Cat and Mouse
10. Pass the Face
12. Funny Face
13. Boom-chicka-boom!
16. Soundscapes
19. Sing-along Word Association

24. Elbow to Elbow
26. Energy Ball
28. Whoosh!
32. Shark Attack!
33. Captain Cod
34. Penguin Race
36. Character Corners
37 Mexican Clap
40. Zip, Zap, Zoom!
41. The Land of Back-to-Front
50. Wolf and Sheep
51. Tableaux
52. 1, 2, 3, Washing Machine!
53. Picture Postcards
54. Star Wars
58. Leap of Faith
60. Family Portraits
64. The Ministry of Funny Walks
65. Emotion Machines
73. Wally's Wallet
79. Living Newspapers
88. Speed Scene
94. Dramategories
98. Instant Opera
100. Pressure Gauge
101. Ring of Trust

Longer Games (15 mins or longer)
16. Soundscapes
17. Human Orchestra
47. Liar, Liar!
51. Tableaux
52. 1, 2, 3, Washing Machine!
58. Leap of Faith
61. Lead With Your…
66. Psychiatrist
67. Object Puppetry Challenge
68. Pauper to Prince
69. Aces High!
71. Max's Motivations
72. Character Hotseat
73. Wally's Wallet
74. Super-sized Stories
76. Hilari-tales
77. The Great Guild of Archaeologists
78. Illustration Station
79. Living Newspapers

82. No, Not Me!
83. Bomb and Shield
85. Why Don't We…
86. Alien Interview
88. Speed Scene
89. Freeze!
90. Cocktail Party
93. Bus-stop Banter
94. Dramategories
95. Death by Chocolate
97. Sit, Stand, Lie Down
98. Instant Opera

Novice Players
1. Rubber Chicken!
2. Greyhound Race
3. MTV Cameraman
4. Super Shake
7. The Incredible Itch
10. Pass the Face
11. Ooey, Gooey, Chewy Gum
12. Funny Face
16. Soundscapes
18. Good Evening, Your Majesty
23. The Amazing 'A's Game
24. Elbow to Elbow
26. Energy Ball
27. Splat!
28. Whoosh!
30. Duck, Duck, Goose!
32. Shark Attack!
33. Captain Cod
34. Penguin Race
37. Mexican Clap
38. Eyes Up!
39. Cyclops
40. Zip, Zap, Zoom!
41. The Land of Back-to-Front
42. Go Bananas!
44. Meddling Monkey
45. The Imaginatively Titled Yes-No Game
46. Colombian Hypnosis
48. Wink Murder
50. Wolf and Sheep
51. Tableaux
52. 1, 2, 3, Washing Machine!
61. Lead With Your…
62. Themed Musical Chairs
63. Grandma's Hat
64. The Ministry of Funny Walks

67. Object Puppetry Challenge
78. Illustration Station
80. Super Chair
81. The Magical Mystery Box
82. No, Not Me!
84. Word Wizard

Pairs and Threes
43. Relay Rhythms
46. Colombian Hypnosis
52. 1, 2, 3, Washing Machine!
57. Friendly Follower
67. Object Puppetry Challenge
70. Slingshot
71. Max's Motivations
72. Character Hotseat
74. Super-sized Stories
85. Why Don't We…
86. Alien Interview
97. Sit, Stand, Lie Down

Requiring Preparation, Props or Music
3. MTV Cameraman
12. Funny Face
14. The Ultimate Tongue-Twisting Challenge
36. Character Corners
37. Mexican Clap
62. Themed Musical Chairs
63. Grandma's Hat
67. Object Puppetry Challenge
69. Aces High!
71. Max's Motivations
73. Wally's Wallet
75. Story Circle
77. The Great Guild of Archaeologists
78. Illustration Station
79. Living Newspapers
80. Super Chair
95. Death by Chocolate
96. Rub-a-dub-dub
98. Instant Opera

Shorter Games (5 mins or less)
1. Rubber Chicken!
2. Greyhound Race
3. MTV Cameraman
4. Super Shake
5. Mirror, Mirror…

Solo Elements

Starting Points for Scene Development

NOTES

NOTES

NOTES